THE BOUNCE

30 Days to a Happier You

THE BOUNCE

30 Days to a Happier You

Let Your Thought Life Create Your New Better Life!

RONALD D. WALTERS

Printed in the United States of America

ISBN 979-8-89114-107-0 (hc)
ISBN 979-8-89114-106-3 (sc)
ISBN 979-8-89114-108-7 (e)

Library of Congress Preassigned Control Number: 2024915612

2024.12.05

MainSpring Books
5901 W. Century Blvd
Suite 750
Los Angeles, CA, US, 90045

www.mainspringbooks.com

I dedicate this book to my wife and lifetime partner, Susanne, the ten beautiful children we share, and all of those who came along through marriage and birth and made our lives a beautiful bounce back.

TABLE OF CONTENTS

PART I: EMPATHY

PART II: EMOTIONS

PART III: INTENTION

PART IV: HATRED

PART V: WORDS

PART I

EMPATHY

THE
BOUNCE

USING TOUGH TIMES TO DEVELOP A SOFT HEART

"Whatever Your Mind Can Conceive and Believe, It Can Achieve."
– NAPOLEON HILL

*"We become what we think about most of the
time, and that's the strangest secret."*
– EARL NIGHTINGALE

As you consider these steps to becoming a happier you, I want to give you a bit of background on my life. I was the youngest in a family of six siblings raised in a small town in Wisconsin. I've experienced various trauma in more than one area during my lifetime. For instance, I have been victimized by bullies and other predators during my early childhood years, by peers and disgruntled classmates through elementary and junior high school, and physically brutalized through violence at the hand of older peers. This trauma continued into my adult years, and each time I was devastated. As I climbed the corporate ladder by succeeding in business and sales, I was disappointed by territorial realignments, lost opportunities resulting from nepotism, and general mistreatment by those who should have otherwise contributed to my success.

Two things that impacted my life early on, to which I credit any success in my present life, were my experience with Jesus Christ at a young age and my personal development through the ministry of God's work! As a young man, I was enthralled with advanced-level basketball players and their incredible energy and focused pre-thought. Their ball handling, court intuition, tenacity, and focus left me mesmerized anytime I watched these talented athletes compete. I was fascinated by their intuitive nature as they moved around the court and their lightning-quick decisions, whether passing, defending, or shooting. I learned that they were so advanced in these skills because of personal discipline and practice, practice, practice. Their minds and bodies worked in complete harmony because they had, for years, prepared for shooting, running, and all other aspects of the game. By the time advanced players competed in a game, they had thousands of hours of dedicated pre-game drills under their belt.

As an example of pre-thought, consider a happy marriage. Focus on the notion of monogamous marriage and meditate on the oneness you can achieve with your spouse. This is a marriage 'pre-thought!' With this paradigm, your marriage will heat up. You'll not waste energy on affairs, fighting, or distancing techniques! The pre-thought of making your marriage great will destroy the paradigm of letting your marriage disintegrate.

As I mentioned, I have endured some difficult times as a human being, yet my life is strangely and wonderfully peaceful and joyous. I credit that outcome to the constant pursuit of prepared thinking or pre-thought! Instinctive decision-making is easier than deliberating over life's complex execution. I have navigated complex issues like a point guard driving to the hoop for an easy lay-up—all due to having the proper mindset.

The ultimate positive change in my life came when my now ex-wife ended a tumultuous marriage by telling me that she would divorce me. At that time, I enjoyed ministerial success with a fast-growing church, business success in the life insurance industry, and meaningful relationships with successful ministers who offered me mentorship and friendship. I didn't realize it at the time, but my divorce was a turning point in my life; it also became an altar upon which I could ultimately thank God for this process and, most importantly, for the people I would meet as a result. I faced financial distress, an anti-male divorce court, and only being allowed to "visit" with my children. I also grappled with an imploding ministerial future because of my own marital problems and the opinions of my ministerial colleagues, while worrying about how this would affect my children and the children of the woman I would choose to partner with in marriage going forward!

I grew from being a latchkey, abandoned child in my early life into a strong, determined, and energetic self-thinker. Still, I had found myself in the throes of a divorce, a debilitating back injury, a subsequent surgery, income loss, and a damaged reputation.

I have felt judged by friends and family about my role in the brokenness my life had become. I am building a successful ministry and growing a family with six biological children and four step-children. I could have ventured into a life of despair from where I was, using every opportunity to become even more embittered, but I chose to become better instead.

This first day of becoming a happier you is celebrating what we call "empathy." Within the pages of this writing are ideas and suggestions from someone who had entered terrible brokenness that culminated with the separation and the divorce of my first marriage decades ago. Most of what you'll read reflects the principles I have utilized to create a much happier version of myself. After all, I spend more time with myself than anybody else!

In your pursuit of empathy, recognize that other people have experienced hardship like yours, have experienced childhood trauma like you, or have had their experience with disillusionment. People have not picked us up but have let us down. I trust you'll enjoy the rest of these writings and surmising from my heart to yours. Here are my thoughts from my morning devotions and the pursuit of trying to be a happier me. I hope you make this a part of your morning devotions as you work to discover a happier YOU!

PRE-THOUGHT:

Through my personal loss and pain, I find the strength to connect with others and foster deeper relationships.

NOTES

PART II

EMOTIONS

THE BOUNCE

THE CONTAGIOUS POWER OF EMOTION

You can tell a lot about how a person feels based on facial expressions, gestures, intonation, and cadence of speech. This focus on the emotional states of others is good, but we also need to pay attention to our own emotions. We often "catch" feelings from those around us. Nicholas Christakis and James Fowler's research shows that happiness can be spread as quickly as a virus. This process is known as "emotional contagion." In 2008 Christakis and Fowler followed 4,739 people for 20 years and surveyed their happiness every few years. They found that an individual's happiness is essentially a ripple effect that flows through social groups to affect those not even connected to the original individual. Additionally, for every reportedly happy person in a group, the joy of each individual in the group goes up by 9%.

Christakis and Fowler's research shows that our happiness is heavily influenced by those around us. However, emotional contagion also occurs with negative emotions, which can be detrimental to our emotion-based close relationships. The anger, stress, or sadness of someone close to us can profoundly affect our moods, and our emotions can impact others just as strongly as if they experienced it themselves. Our brains deal with second-hand emotions as if they were our own. Negative emotions can lead to deeper health issues such as heart disease. Second-hand stress can also create rifts in our relationships with our loved ones. Unfortunately, it's easier to "catch" negative emotions than positive ones, and people who are generally more sensitive to the feelings of others are more susceptible to emotional contagion. [9] Negative emotions like stress and anger destroy our brains' judgment and memory portions. Continuous anger can severely affect personal relationships and job performance. [5]

THE PASTOR'S PERSPECTIVE

Sometimes individuals believe they have a "right" to be pessimistic. They let their negative emotions and thought processes run wild! The article above concludes that unhappiness breeds unhappiness, depression breeds depression, and anger breeds anger! You may feel a right to spray your negativity and spread your emotional contagion to the people around you, but recognize how unhealthy your virus of negativity affects those around you.

You might stay at home, coughing and sneezing from inside your little world of hurt, and still expose your spouse, children, acquaintances, and business partners to a virus that can bring even significant corporations to their knees. Think of that adverse effect going into your children's ears or your spouse's heart, whom you agreed to love, honor, and cherish. According to the larger scientific population, I cause stress to my children, marriage, and social groups if I decide to be angry. If I choose to be depressed, I can easily set in motion the depression of my entire family. It is selfish and ignorant to allow myself to impose negative consequences on my children and vicariously on my grandchildren.

"Be careful for nothing, but in every thing by prayer and supplication with thanksgiving let your requests be made known unto God. And the peace of God, which passeth all understanding, shall keep your hearts and minds through Christ Jesus. Finally, brethren, whatsoever things are true, whatsoever things are honest, whatsoever things are just, whatsoever things are pure, whatsoever things are lovely, whatsoever things are of good report; if there be any virtue, and if there be any praise, think on these things. Those things, which ye have both learned, and received, and heard, and seen in me, do: and the God of peace shall be with you." (Philippians 4:6-9 KJV)

If I choose to give the gift of God's peace to my spouse, my children, and heirs that follow for many generations. Because of my controlled emotions, they will receive a gift allowing them to live in happiness and contentment throughout the ages. Through Christ, I, myself, can accomplish this gift.

Meditate on and believe in the word of God that your life is good with proper pre-thought. Your life shall become that gift, and you shall become a positive emotional contagion to the little ones. Come on, Christian, start right now! Stop the negativity and start releasing God through your thoughts to provide yourself with an expected positive life. Those close to you will thank you.

PRE-THOUGHT:

Recognizing that emotions are contagious, I choose to embody an exuberant happiness that inspires those around me.

NOTES

THE BOUNCE

ANXIETY

To understand anxiety, we first need to understand cognition. Cognition is the mental action or process of acquiring knowledge and understanding through thought, experience, and the senses. Put simply, cognition is how we understand the world around us and interpret how the world affects us. [42] When our brain incorrectly interprets the world, our body responds with panic. If this occurs regularly and consistently, especially if it interferes with our ability to perform our daily routine, it can be diagnosed as a panic disorder. Panic disorder strikes without reason or warning, causing sudden fear, anxiety attacks, and physical symptoms such as a racing heart. [29]

Most people feel small amounts of anxiety in regular life, which can even be beneficial. Anxiety disorders, however, cause such a high level of stress that individuals no longer have the ability to lead a normal life. Anxiety disorders involve not only feelings of fear but also physiological effects like an increased heart rate, sweating, or even blurry vision. An anxiety disorder can be diagnosed if the response is inappropriate for the situation, if it can not be controlled, or interferes with normal functioning.

Types of anxiety disorders include the following:

- ✓ Panic Disorder, where intense feelings of terror occur suddenly and, often, without reason;
- ✓ Post-traumatic Stress Disorder (PTSD), which develops after an intensely stressful event;
- ✓ Social Anxiety Disorder, or a fear of social interactions;
- ✓ Specific Phobias or fears about a particular object or situation;
- ✓ Generalized Anxiety Disorder, which is intense, unprovoked worry.

Anxiety disorders are the most common form of diagnosable mental illness and affect more women than men. The precise cause is still unknown, but anxiety disorders are most likely caused by chemical imbalances in the brain. [6]

THE PASTOR'S PERSPECTIVE

KEY VERSES

- "He also that received seed among the thorns is he that heareth the word; and the care of this world, and the deceitfulness of riches, choke the word, and he becometh unfruitful." (Matthew 13:22 KJV)
- "Therefore remove sorrow from thy heart, and put away evil from thy flesh: for childhood and youth are vanity." (Ecclesiastes 11:10 KJV).
- "Take no thought for your life, what ye shall eat; neither for the body, what ye shall put on. The life is more than meat, and the body is more than raiment." (Luke 12:22-23 KJV)
- "Fear thou not; for I am with thee: be not dismayed; for I am thy God: I will strengthen thee; yea, I will help thee; yea, I will uphold thee with the right hand of my righteousness." (Isaiah 41:10 KJV)
- "Be anxious for nothing, but in everything by prayer and supplication, with thanksgiving, let your requests be made known to God." (Philippians 4:6 NASB)

Again, science provides why the God who created you offered a "word" that speaks directly to handling what has become a regular part of the human experience, the emotion of anxiety! A guiding principle that I have used in my life is, "I cannot control what happens to me. I can only control what happens in me." I have a steadfast and unmovable opinion because I must keep my emotions free of clutter, which typically remains in the human mind. I've tried to love God, prioritize relationships around me, love people, and then go about doing business, so I can provide for others. Where is the harm in that? However, I have noticed people will do and say all manner of evil against me. I experienced physical abuse in my childhood and emotional abuse in my adulthood. Still, I'm just trying to be me at the end of the day! Therefore, I have learned the same lesson as every other human through experience. I have gone through a divorce, and I have needed to speak to a therapist. I have experienced and still experience pain, suffering, and anxiety.

Early in my adulthood, I became a Christian, and I began to trust something other than people, but I still had to live with people and get along with them. However, I am not required to trust what people in my life say is or will be valid. Instead, I know they speak words and show actions to me from their perception of how the world is to them. For example, if I encounter a judgmental person who may not like something about me, I am not required to perceive myself in the same way they do. Positive pre-thought about myself becomes a defense against the temptation to perceive myself through the eyes of another person's judgment.

Christians have a significant advantage, as we can see ourselves through the Word of God. Our loving father says through love that, without Christ, I am a sinner and, as a sinner, need repentance. When I was exposed to this truth rather than self-justification, I sought the Word to discover why God would think I needed repentance. By seeking the Word, I found I needed to repent for the things that my sin had left inside of me. I also had to repent for what others tried to attach to me through their actions, facial expressions, angry words, and distractions created by their judgmental nature.

Through studying the Word, I now understand that unpleasant experiences with angry and judgmental people show me their way of speaking to me from their personal experiences and how they saw me. Those negative experiences could have been devastating to my self-worth without a proper self-sense of who I am through Christ. By knowing Him and His Word, I now see myself through His paradigm and live in the "newness of life." With this paradigm as my pre-thought, I am far less prone to anxiety, panic attacks, and terrible thoughts and accusations toward those close to me, and I can live in the realm of "God's peace and joy." As a pastor, I hope you have this same kind of worry-free living through a self-image built through a pre-thought life based on the Word of the Lord. A Christ-centered pre-thought will empower you to choose whether you accept the opinions of others in the world as a definition of who you are or if you take the opinion of God and grow to be who He has called you to be.

At this time, meditate on the verses mentioned above. Take note of Ecclesiastes 11:10, where the central message is to literally forgive childhood. Recognizing the word of God calls us to forgive what happened to us in early life. Impress into your heart the cross of Christ. Notice where He said, "Father forgive them, for they do not know what they do." On Easter Sunday, where we all think about the great sacrifice Jesus made on the cross. Only a few of us really celebrate HIS three days in the tomb. This time of year gives me hope because he was resurrected from the dead. It is possible to emerge from the tomb of childhood fear or adult anxiety. Then, you can begin to put into people the things you glean from God's Word. Instead of those things that you have gathered through a life of pain and suffering. It is time you rise and walk in the way Christ called you!

If you allow anxiety, missed thoughts, and panic attacks to define the existence you choose on Earth, you will affect those around you like a virus. Let's put anxiety under the blood of Jesus! Forgive the people around us, forgive what we have allowed to happen inside of us, and rise and walk through the work of the cross into this world with joy and peace. Come on, Christian, love the people around you, don't judge them, and don't hurt them with your thoughts and actions. Right now, choose to create an atmosphere of love, peace, and joy. Then, you're going to become the solution instead of adding to the continual problematic issues of the human experience! Remember Paul said, "Forgetting those things behind, I press toward the mark of the high calling in Christ!" You are to be resurrected from the tomb into a new life with God from the death of sin.

Truckers used to say, "Hey, good buddy, got your ears on?" I say now, "Do you have ears on to hear what the Spirit is saying to you?"

PRE-THOUGHT:

I will no longer allow my thoughts to fuel my emotions; instead, I will cultivate a mindset that promotes calm and positivity.

NOTES

THE BOUNCE

TRUST

When it comes to trusting others, people typically fall into one of two categories: distrusting or overly trusting. Those who distrust tend to assume the worst in others and keep them at a distance so they won't be disappointed. Conversely, those who over-trust tend to believe the best in others and are shocked when someone breaks that trust. We need to find a balance between the two extremes. Trust should be gained not only by words but by actions. There are a few qualities to look at when deciding to trust a new person. First, trustworthy people will have open and honest communication about how they are feeling. Hiding feelings leads to resentment in any relationship. Second, trustworthy people will create physical, emotional, or virtual boundaries. The violation of boundaries causes disrespect in the relationship. Third, trustworthy people are reliable in their promises. Breaking promises causes disappointment in the relationship. Finally, trustworthy people are predictable in their actions. Unpredictable behaviors cause doubt in the relationship. Learning to trust others is primarily about listening to your own intuition and knowledge. [22]

THE PASTOR'S PERSPECTIVE

A particular biblical concept that is important for human beings to understand before entering into any and all human relationships.

Romans 3:3-4 says:

"For what if some did not believe? Shall their unbelief make the faith of God without effect? God forbid: yea, let God be true, but every man a liar; as it is written, That thou mightest be justified in thy sayings, and mightest overcome when thou art judged." *(KJV)*

Consider what David wrote in Psalms. He was just a king of many, many people. What did he know? David knew he could choose to either trust or mistrust God. How David overcame his personal life as a King would have been impossible if he did not understand an essential truth. All human beings have failure built into them, but we can trust God. The foundation of this truth makes it okay for me to get to know people, accept those people as they are, and possibly enjoy a continuous relationship with those people while I am living on this earth. Let's take a look at a few Psalms.

KEY VERSES

- *"Shiggaion of David, which he sang unto the LORD, concerning the words of Cush the Benjamite. O LORD my God, in thee do I put my trust: save me from all them that persecute me, and deliver me."* *(Psalms 7:1 KJV)*
- *"And they that know thy name will put their trust in thee: for thou, LORD, hast not forsaken them that seek thee."* *(Psalms 9:10 KJV)*
- *"Trust in the LORD, and do good; [so] shalt thou dwell in the land, and verily thou shalt be fed."* *(Psalms 37:3 KJV)*
- *"Commit thy way unto the LORD; trust also in him; and he shall bring [it] to pass."* *(Psalms 37:5 KJV)*
- *"And the LORD shall help them, and deliver them: he shall deliver them from the wicked, and save them because they trust in him."* *(Psalms 37:40 KJV)*

David gave us a fundamental principle; God is trustworthy and should be the one entity that I place my personal trust in. God is my defender, redeemer, and deliverer. People will let me down, but the Lord will always sustain me. If my trust is in God, and I spend my earthly time getting to know Him through study, devotions, prayer, and personal and community worship, I feel 'safe.' He is my priority relationship since I find comfort, direction, instruction, and righteousness within the context of my trust in the Lord. He is the one to make all things right if I am mistreated by those around me. I don't have to judge the people around me because He is their judge. I only have to love the people around me because He is my judge.

When my trust is placed in God, I can love people no matter what their behaviors try to make me think about them. If my trust is only in people who say they love God, I blame God when they disappoint me. However, if my trust is accurately placed solely in the Lord, people's actions are less influential in developing my trust. Trust allows me as a person to have peace and enjoy every day to the fullest. I've learned that all people are a disappointment at one time or another. I can also say that my Lord has never once been a disappointment with all my heart. I'd rather trust that God is true and recognize that every person who walks the earth has the potential to lie, mistreat, abandon, and even not truly love me. That is the human experience, where these things happen to every person and almost every relationship. To myself, I have had to say, "Get over it!"

The word of God says all people are going to fail. It also tells us that, in all situations, God never fails. Trust in the Lord is the foundation of all pre-thought. I can expect to be disappointed by those around me. Yet, I expect to never be disappointed by the God within me. He has asked me to trust Him. He can also ask me to "love [my] enemies" because my trust in Him will compensate me for the pain and sorrow I received from those enemies. My trust is in God. Therefore, He can ask me to "take up my cross and follow Him" because nothing reflects the brokenness man gives to others more than what we did to Him on the cross. I can trust this God who walked among us with love the whole time, knowing we would crucify Him with hate.

I trust in God because I know that, to enjoy my human experience, I must love all of those around me who, according to the word, are "liars"! Plainly, Jesus said of himself, "I am the Way, the truth, the life."

Come on, Christian! Put your trust in God and release everyone else to be human, so you can fill your brief time on earth with love, joy, peace, gentleness, meekness, self-control, goodness, and faith!

PRE-THOUGHT:

To cultivate happiness with others, I must embrace trust. So, I'll let my past bad experiences take a backseat.

NOTES

THE BOUNCE

SADNESS

From an early age, we learn to avoid sad feelings. Crying children are silenced and told, "It's okay, you're fine," which teaches them that being sad is bad or wrong. Children don't have the vocabulary to describe their feelings. Still, they will remember the emotions, and the feelings will affect them for the rest of their lives. The caregivers' job is to help children develop ways to express and deal with their emotions. Sadness differs from depression in that sadness is a natural response to life events and experiences. Depression, on the other hand, often happens without warning or explanation. Depression suppresses other emotions so that we feel no emotions. Sadness, however, helps us see what we value most in life. According to psychologist Robert Firestone, "When we feel sadness, it centers us" [13]. Depression often makes us scared that feeling sad will release all of the emotions that have been suppressed. The feeling-suppressing methods we develop as children are often detrimental to our adult lives. Psychologist Lisa Firestone says, "We can't selectively numb pain without numbing joy" [14]. Suppressing sadness makes us less likely to be truly happy.

THE PASTOR'S PERSPECTIVE

"But when the young man heard that saying, he went away sorrowful: for he had great possessions." (Matthew 19:22 KJV)

Consider the first example of sorrow in the rich young ruler who "had great possessions." For this discussion, this could be either material things or, for most of us who lack material wealth, it can reflect our emotional baggage. The word "possessions" in Matthew 19 refers to "the estates" or things passed down. In perfect families, they are positive personality traits, attributes, and habits in a young person. However, in an abusive or dysfunctional family, baggage can bring sorrow. A significant quantity of depressive and sorrowful inventory is the memory of hurt, disappointments, abuse, neglect, and other painful human experiences.

"And they were exceeding sorrowful, and began every one of them to say unto him, Lord, is it I?" (Matthew 26:22 KJV)

For our discussion, those in Matthew 26 were sorrowful because they had the revelation that one would betray the Lord. In our lifetime, when we have forsaken righteousness or willingly entered into sinful behaviors, we have knowingly allowed ourselves to betray Christ inside of us.

Jesus was right there in the room with the disciples. They were in the "presence" of the mighty God in Christ yet still felt sorrow at the revelation of their personal potential to betray the person they loved. Think of someone who has betrayed you in this life and brought your heart to a place of sorrow. A parent, romantic partner, teacher, coach, or peer? Whatever caused you to betray Jesus, repentance should ease your sorrowful heart.

KEY VERSES

- *"And he took with him Peter and the two sons of Zebedee and began to be sorrowful and very heavy. Then saith he unto them, My soul is exceeding sorrowful, even unto death: tarry ye here, and watch with me."* (Matthew 26:37 KJV)
- *"For his anger endureth but a moment; in his favour is life: weeping may endure for a night, but joy cometh in the morning."* (Psalms 30:5 KJV)

The Matthew 26 example of sorrow reflects the words of Jesus Christ when he felt the weight of the decision to go to the cross. It's impossible to understand what He felt because we are not the savior. We know that when He was the closest to fulfilling the divine call upon His life, there was a weight upon His heart that He described as "sorrowful unto death." What a sublime godly moment each of us can have when we allow ourselves to become Christian. Some think that this entrance into a new life is filled with nothing but joy and happiness. Yet, Isaiah describes the Savior as "a man of sorrow and acquainted with grief." Why would we want to have a life outside of what He felt? The balance of our life comes when we can steward sorrow and joy, sometimes on the same day. This good/bad, high/low scenario provides us with an opportunity to be human and Christian. To be without sorrow and the feeling of despair, we can never truly understand "the joy of the Lord is my strength." If we have sorrow and emotional pain in life, that experience of those emotions provides us with celebration when we are free from them and rise above those circumstances.

To meditate on the reality that life is challenging is a healthy thing to do. However, I don't stay there or let it be the foundation of my life. According to those three scriptures above, taking inventory of all the hurts and blessings can become a "great estate." Therefore, I need to let go and give the testimony of victory to the poor. I know the thought I have betrayed the Lord brings sorrow into my life, provoking me to celebrate when I haven't broken His heart! The choice of going to the cross to follow Him can be tough to navigate, but come on, Christian! Lay down the usual reactions to the sorrow of life, take up your cross, and follow Him into the joy of building His church! He is with you, loves you, and knows about sorrow, but He gives us "victory"!

PRE-THOUGHT:

Temporary sadness does not signify failure. I choose to welcome joy after allowing myself to feel and process my emotions.

NOTES

HAPPINESS

The science of happiness is the study of what makes people happy. Positive psychology branches off from the study of happiness to a specific type of psychology and therapy that emphasizes the development of positive emotions. Happiness is one of the most widely researched and discussed feelings. These studies show how our thoughts and actions affect our happiness and outline the habits of truly happy people. For example, happy people regularly exercise and eat healthy foods, which comes from an understanding that eating healthy foods and exercising can significantly improve one's mood. Therefore, happy people are physically and emotionally well. Happy people have open and honest relationships with those around them. They participate in "active-constructive responding" or express genuine interest in others' emotions and feelings and respond encouragingly. Happy people perform acts of kindness whether they know the person or not. They cultivate an atmosphere of kindness around them. Happy people have a "flow." They have motivation for what they are doing because they enjoy it. Happy people find deep meaning in their life. They use a connection to religion or their spirit to give their life a deeper meaning. Happy people use their strengths and live by their virtues. They use traits and aspects that are unique to them to achieve their goals. Happy people have high regard for gratitude and hope. They know that being grateful leads to other positive emotions. [32]

THE PASTOR'S PERSPECTIVE

To be a happy person, grow honest relationships through acts of kindness, be physically well, flow with spiritual meaning while working on your strengths, and show gratitude.

In our study, seven categories outline the habits of happy people. These practices should help us to "rejoice in the Lord always"! and were established for Christians, especially those involved in a church community. They will not only verify but strengthen these patterns in our daily life. Consider number one: having honest relationships and close friendships. It is better to develop close friendships with those who have genuinely acknowledged that Jesus is the Lord, have repented of a lifestyle of sin, and are doing their best to live patterns of holiness.

Regarding acts of kindness, Galatians 6:10 says,

- *"Do good unto all men, especially unto them who are of the household of faith." The ideas of exercise and finding a flow into the more profound meaning and spiritual activity pretty much sum up the notion of, "Clap your hands, all you people, and shout unto God with the voice of triumph come before his presence with singing and praise him with the dance and timbrel"* (Psalm 47:1).

As far as being grateful, "Come before his presence with thanksgiving and into his courts with praise!" (Psalm 100). We are taught to revere and honor leadership by communicating well with them. It is strange to me when people don't see the value of a church community and don't fight for unity in the bond of love.

I once heard a story about a stepfather who owned a ranch out west but wanted to mine for gold in California. He hastily sold his ranch to move to the West Coast, where he began to excavate a small, little claim. Sometime within the first year, he recognized that the land he had purchased in California, with the fee from the land he sold, would yield to him very little gold. However, the ranch he sold had a great harvest of petroleum underneath the soil. The person who bought the property that the stepfather ran away from could cash in, while the stepfather sought gold and riches elsewhere. The stepfather ultimately felt the pain of a deal gone awry.

Some Christians are like the man who sold his petroleum-rich farm for a worthless lot of land somewhere else. We become lonely, sad, and perhaps even angry at people that seem to be living within the context of Christianity throughout a vibrant church community by isolating and pulling back from biblical mandates and patterns of involvement with others and friendships. Self-imposed exile only fosters anti-happy practices. Put down your pout, overcome your fear, enter into fellowship with the body of Christ, and you will find the seven habits of happy people. David in Psalms says, "Blessed is the man that walketh not in the counsel of the ungodly, nor standeth in the way of sinners, nor sitteth in the seat of the scornful. But his delight is in the law of the Lord, and in his law doth he meditate day and night."

 Come on, you Christian, let your love show and prosper as you prospect the gold where you are planted.

PRE-THOUGHT:

Happy is how I choose to be, not the place where I have chosen to live.

NOTES

DISGUST

Children must be taught disgust. Babies have an automatic response to distasteful food. However, there is no emotion behind this response; it is simply a sensory reaction. Studies have shown that babies will try to eat fake dog poop made out of peanut butter and stinky cheese. Children typically begin to show disgust around age six. This propensity for aversion increases throughout adolescence and decreases into adulthood. We usually learn disgust from those around us. However, there is evidence that we are intrinsically disgusted by insects and bugs. [23]

Disgust is essential because it can tell us how our environment affects us. Disgust keeps us from getting sick by preventing us from eating rotten or poisonous foods. Similarly, disgust keeps us away from toxic people who have betrayed our trust or abused us. Validating others' disgust can decrease the anxiety and shame they feel. Disgust can be an outward physical or an internal emotional sensation. Processing the disgust we feel will help our brain return to a neutral state. [18]

If you were given a choice between three glasses of water—one with a bitter taste, one with arsenic, and one that had had dog poop in it but had been filtered—which would you drink? Psychology professor Paul Rozin performed a trial with a similar setup to this question. According to Rozin, disgust is based on the "knowledge of the nature of something," not necessarily the fear of sickness. Rozin found that people were less disgusted with the arsenic glass than with the filtered water glass. There is a stark difference between fear and disgust. Fear is the reaction to harmful effects on our physical selves, while disgust is the reaction to the harmful impacts on our souls. Researchers agree on three criteria that, when combined, will make something a "core disgust."

To be a "core disgust," the object must be "something you could eat, something that has or had a life of its own, and something that has the power to make other things disgusting." This final criterion is, perhaps, the most central. If you didn't like carrots but were given a bowl of mashed potatoes that a carrot had fallen in and was taken out, you would still likely eat it. However, if a bug had fallen in and was taken out, you would consider the bowl "contaminated." The phrase, "Once in contact, always in contact," similarly applies to situations with food or objects. Still, it can also apply to people who commit immoral acts. These are called sociomoral disgusts. One such example is cannibalistic serial killers in Western culture. Most serial killers are seen as despicable, but they become disgusting once they decide to eat their victims. Sociomoral disgusts also vary around the world. For example, compared to people in the west, people in India are less disgusted by core disgusts but much more disgusted by sociomoral disgusts. [10]

THE PASTOR'S PERSPECTIVE

In the study of emotions, it is exciting to me how science has related disgust to a level of scorn. The Bible has a lot to say about scorners and scorning. Please read each of the following biblical examples of this lesson:

KEY VERSES

- *"But when Sanballat the Horonite, and Tobiah the servant, the Ammonite, and Geshem the Arabian, heard it, they laughed us to scorn, and despised us, and said, What is this thing that ye do? will ye rebel against the king?"* (Nehemiah 2:19 KJV)

  - *"And he thought scorn to lay hands on Mordecai alone; for they had showed him the people of Mordecai: wherefore Haman sought to destroy all the Jews that were throughout the whole kingdom of Ahasuerus, even the people of Mordecai."* (Esther 3:6 KJV)
  - *"I am as one mocked of his neighbour, who calleth upon God, and he answereth him: the just upright man is laughed to scorn."* (Job 12:4 KJV)

- *"My friends scorn me: but mine eye poureth out tears unto God."* (Job 16:20 KJV)
- *"The righteous see it, and are glad: and the innocent laugh them to scorn."* (Job 22:19 KJV)
- *"What man is like Job, who drinketh up scorning like water?"* (Job 34:7 KJV)
- *"He scorneth the multitude of the city, neither regardeth he the crying of the driver."* (Job 39:7 KJV)
- *"We are become a reproach to our neighbours, a scorn and derision to them that are round about us."* (Psalms 79:4 KJV)
- *"Blessed is the man that walketh not in the counsel of the ungodly, nor standeth in the way of sinners, nor sitteth in the seat of the scornful."* (Psalms 1:1 KJV)
- *"But thou art holy, O thou that inhabitest the praises of Israel. Our fathers trusted in thee: they trusted, and thou didst deliver them. They cried unto thee and were delivered: they trusted in thee and were not confounded. But I am a worm and no man; a reproach of men, and despised of the people. All they that see me laugh me to scorn: they shoot out the lip, they shake the head, saying, He trusted on the Lord that he would deliver him: let him deliver him, seeing he delighted in him."* (Psalms 22:3-8 - KJV)
- *"Thou makest us a reproach to our neighbours, a scorn and a derision to them that are round about us."* (Psalms 44:13 KJV)
- *"Our soul is exceedingly filled with the scorning of those that are at ease, and with the contempt of the proud."* (Psalms 123:4 KJV)
- *"How long, ye simple ones, will ye love simplicity? and the scorners delight in their scorning, and fools hate knowledge?"* (Proverbs 1:22 KJV)
- *"Surely he scorneth the scorners: but he giveth grace unto the lowly."* (Proverbs 3:34 KJV)
- *"He that reproveth a scorner getteth to himself shame: and he that rebuketh a wicked man getteth himself a blot."* (Proverbs 9:7 KJV)
- *"Reprove not a scorner, lest he hate thee: rebuke a wise man, and he will love thee."* (Proverbs 9:8 KJV)
- *"If thou be wise, thou shalt be wise for thyself: but if thou scornest, thou alone shalt bear it."* (Proverbs 9:12 KJV)
- *"A wise son heareth his father's instruction: but a scorner heareth not rebuke."* (Proverbs 13:1 KJV)
- *"A scorner seeketh wisdom, and findeth it not: but knowledge is easy unto him that understandeth."* (Proverbs 14:6 KJV)
- *"A scorner loveth not one that reproveth him: neither will he go unto the wise."* (Proverbs 15:12 KJV)
- *"Smite a scorner, and the simple will beware: and reprove one that hath understanding, and he will understand knowledge."* (Proverbs 19:25 KJV)
- *"An ungodly witness scorneth judgment: and the mouth of the wicked devoureth iniquity."* (Proverbs 19:28 KJV)

- *"Judgments are prepared for scorners, and stripes for the back of fools."* (Proverbs 19:29 KJV)
- *"When the scorner is punished, the simple is made wise: and when the wise is instructed, he receiveth knowledge."* (Proverbs 21:11 KJV)
- *"Proud and haughty scorner is his name, who dealeth in proud wrath."* (Proverbs 21:24 KJV)
- *"Cast out the scorner, and contention shall go out; yea, strife and reproach shall cease."* (Proverbs 22:10 KJV)
- *"The thought of foolishness is sin: and the scorner is an abomination to men."* (Proverbs 24:9 KJV)

Scorning, according to science, is likened to disgust. In the word of God, it indicates that when a person begins to scorn, there are four dynamics;

1. The preached word and the judgment of Godly instruction cause an emotional knee-jerk reaction. The scornful person then develops a "hatred" for the preacher, not just the preached word.A scornful person causes disunity, which is common among those who hate the kingdom of heaven. A scornful person lives in contention and shares contention whenever they can.

2. A scornful person withdraws from those who have proven wisdom and understanding. They find their light in the pathology of hate and distrust rather than delight in the law of the Lord, as a scornful person spends very little time studying the word of God.

3. The scorner fights the works of God in a community by calling out for civic authorities or the government to intimidate what they consider the work of the 'feeble' people of God.

As you look through the scripture, you'll notice sinners can repent, and the ungodly can change their ways, but scorners never seem to rise from a place called "the seat of the scornful" (Psalm 1:1 KJV). Scorning appears to become a pathology that allows scorners to think of themselves above the preached word and live outside of the parameters of biblical discipline. Scorners may say they appreciate the leaders, but they withdraw and want to spend less time in the presence of the Lord. When the preaching of the word comes across the pulpit, scorners have disgust for it and for the person delivering it.

One of the simple joys that I have in life is I'm somewhat beyond being concerned with people's opinions. I recognize I'm moving toward an appointment with death and, after that, the judgment. Therefore, I need to preach the Word as given, not as it would be well received. Since in the heart of man, there's very little we find in common with the Word of God. The Word of God is constantly moving His people to higher places and locations of the greater revelation of self! The Word is about a psychological phenomenon known as disgust, which provokes secularists to the power of scorning.

Please take a minute to measure what's in your heart. How do you respond to the preaching of God's Word? That reaction will be the same as how you will react in the presence of Jesus Christ Himself at the white throne of judgment. If you find being around other Christians on this side of death difficult, what makes you think He would let you live with Christians on the other side of eternity? Rejecting His decisions for our eternal placement is like sitting in the church and scorning those trying to live for God. Those who are preaching the word of God and those who are trying to love you through Jesus.

Come on, Christian! Don't sit, shake your head, or laugh under your breath at what we are attempting to do in the name of Jesus. Why do such things? Repent and enjoy the body of Christ. Let's all move toward victory together!

PRE-THOUGHT:

I refuse to be consumed by scorn. Instead, I will release the things that weigh me down and bring me sorrow.

NOTES

THE BOUNCE

SURPRISE

Researchers have only recently begun to understand the science behind why surprise brings us pleasure. When we are given surprise gifts, our brain's pleasure center receives dopamine, which floods our bodies with a comfortable feeling. That shot of dopamine makes our brain want more of whatever elicited it in the first place, making us want more surprises. Dopamine increases attraction and excitement, which then improves our romantic relationships. Since surprise shows us something we do not know, it can help our brain make new neural pathways with new information. Our brains are designed to enjoy new stimuli. When we experience something new, our brain releases a shot of pleasure-inducing dopamine.

Additionally, surprise heightens our happiness from good surprises, making the sadness felt with negative surprises even more devastating. Surprise helps our brain focus our attention on new stimuli. This is likely due to the brain releasing a shot of noradrenaline, which activates our fight-or-flight response. The repeated dopamine release during surprises has also been measured to reduce anxiety and depression. The most beneficial type of surprise is awe which we  feel when we see something impressive or powerful. Being in awe has been measured to decrease inflammatory chemicals in our bodies. [19]

THE PASTOR'S PERSPECTIVE

When did walking with God become boring? Think precisely about when you lost your excitement about His presence, His people, and more importantly, when did you lose the <u>awe</u> at His word?

Please read each of the following biblical examples in this lesson:

KEY VERSES

- *"The fear [<u>awe</u>] of the Lord is the beginning of wisdom: and the knowledge of the holy is understanding."* (Proverbs 9:10 KJV)
- *"But unto you that fear [<u>awe</u>] my name shall the Sun of righteousness arise with healing in his wings; and ye shall go forth, and grow up as calves of the stall."* (Malachi 4:2 KJV)
- *"Let us hear the conclusion of the whole matter: Fear [<u>awe</u>] God, and keep his commandments: for this is the whole duty of man."* (Ecclesiastes 12:13 KJV)
- *"Praise ye the Lord. Blessed is the man that feareth [<u>stand in awe</u>] of the Lord, that delighteth greatly in his commandments."* (Psalms 112:1 KJV)
- *"O that there were such a heart in them, that they would fear [<u>be in awe of</u>] me, and keep all my commandments always, that it might be well with them, and with their children forever!"* (Deuteronomy 5:29 KJV)

In the puniness of our thinking, we consider the idea of fearing the Lord as us being in a position where we should run and hide from God because 'He's going to get us.' We feel that because we are on the wrong side of the relationship. We think He will get us because we do not truly understand His nature, nor do we desire to be excited about or surprised by Him or His actions.

A relationship that has lost the 'awe' can be described as a boring relationship lacking intellectual stimulation. Thus, the relationship has become less valuable and much less rewarding to those in that boring relationship. We know that the Word became flesh and dwelt among us. We understand that we are to have a relationship with the Word as it manifests in the form of a physical person. Then, it would stand to reason that our relationship with God has the potential to become dull, unstimulating, and, therefore, not fulfilling at all. The opposite is true; it can be stimulating, exciting, and highly fulfilling. The choice is up to you.

If we have a relationship with a member of the opposite gender, and they send us a note that tells us that they find us attractive or want a relationship with us, we will put that love letter in a safe place because we will likely want to go back and read it over and over. We find that written communication from the admirer to be exciting no matter how many times we've read over it. However, the Christian who has the very word of God at their disposal daily fails to pursue it because we no longer have any awe for the writer of the love letter. Our perception of our heavenly Father is that 'He is so controlling.' In our finite minds, we have lost the excitement of discovering what His infinite mind reveals in His word, and we have become bored. We quickly move away from His word and begin to trust the excitement of what the Bible calls "the world." 1 John 2:15 says, "Love not the world, neither the things that are in the world. If any man loves the world, the love of the Father is not in him". This does not mean that the Father stops loving. It is almost as if God could become the "prodigal father" to spend all of His love on those with no deep relationship. More likely, we have become the prodigal lover and are bored with this God who paints a different sunrise every morning and brings a different sensation to our physical body through cold wind. The joy of warmth comes from the sun He created. Through the book of Revelation, John wrote that if we lose our "first love" for God and the joy of being surprised by God, He develops "ought" against us (Revelation 2:4).

The government-imposed social isolation showed us where our excitement lies in relation to what thrills us. When a Christian is born of water and spirit, there's <u>awe</u> and excitement about God's creations. We can't get enough of his word or His presence. Early in our relationship, we might even have had a prayer life. All of this is because we were excited about this new relationship with a very stable and sure God. I heard a wise preacher say that if something in your relationship with God has changed, it is not God!

Are you bored with marriage? You're probably bored with the giver of marriage, who is God! Tired of child-rearing? Perhaps you've lost your <u>awe</u> of God and no longer want to raise these children to serve a "boring" Lord. Not teaching your neighbors how much God loves them? You're allowing them to teach you how much excitement the world has. Let's fall in love with Jesus and never lose the surprise factor He wants to give us through His word and daily actions.

If the world and the things of the world are where your excitement is, I recommend you divorce entertainment and remove your flirtation with lascivious and carnal pursuits. My dear friend, He shows His handiwork and lets us know that He's on the way back. Do not forget, though! He's looking for a bride, an eternal lover. She is surprised by the beautiful sunrise painting and comforted in the warmth of brand-new mercy every day. Moving from where you

rise after a night of sleep into a world that needs you to point out how awesome our heavenly lover is. Come on, Christian, you've got this.

PRE-THOUGHT:

Embrace the journey of life by staying enthusiastic about your faith in God.

NOTES

THE BOUNCE

ANTICIPATION

When you anticipate something, you think or do something about it before it happens. The feeling of anticipation helps us lead happier lives. A 2007 study by Van Boven and Ashworth compared the excitement people felt when looking forward to things or looking back at them. They asked participants to think about both past and future vacations. Overall, they measured more excitement when the participants thought about possible future vacations, likely because "We have an expectation that future events will make us feel more emotional than ones that have passed." We tend to talk more about things in the future we are excited about than things that have already happened. [35]

Neil Patel has three important psychological points about anticipation that can help us interact and understand others. First, Patel states that people anticipate happy experiences. Since our brain is always on, we cannot stop it from anticipating what's next. When anticipation happens, the brain receives a dose of dopamine which stimulates happiness. Research shows that our brains are designed to anticipate positive events. Second, our past experiences shape how we expect future events to happen, also known as "perceptual anticipation." Research shows that stimuli  are the cause, whether the results of past events, instructions on future tasks, or similarities between past and present events. Last, anticipation decreases when we're stressed. Our brain tries to get rid of stress by adaptation or avoidance. Adapting to stress releases dopamine, which leads to feelings of happiness. [30]

THE PASTOR'S PERSPECTIVE

KEY VERSES

- *"For as many as are led by the Spirit of God, they are the sons of God. For ye have not received the spirit of bondage again to fear; but ye have received the Spirit of adoption, whereby we cry, Abba, Father. The Spirit itself beareth witness with our spirit that we are the children of God: And if children, then heirs; heirs of God, and joint-heirs with Christ; if so be that we suffer with him, that we may be also glorified together. For I reckon that the sufferings of this present time are not worthy to be compared with the glory which shall be revealed in us. For the earnest expectation of the creature waiteth for the manifestation of the sons of God."* (Romans 8:14-19 KJV)
- *"And not only they, but ourselves also, which have the first fruits of the Spirit, even we ourselves groan within ourselves, waiting for the adoption, to wit, the redemption of our body. For we are saved by hope: but hope that is seen is not hope: for what a man seeth, why doth he yet hope for?"* (Romans 8:23-24 KJV)

Hope for the sake of this last look at the earthly emotion of anticipation. Psychologists and professional marketers agree that anticipation deals with the hope that our subsequent experiences will be positive. They say that this mindset of anticipation comes from healthy past experiences. People who are constantly anticipating bad, sad, or traumatic experiences can suffer a form of mental illness. Like any other part of the body, the mind is subject to disease, contagions, and influences from outside of our body, very similar to the different aspects and systems of being human. If our digestive system experiences a bug, we are ready to discharge from our gut everything we have eaten because the bug makes us feel sick. Developing a brain bug such as a painful experience or traumatic event robs us of what the apostle wrote in Romans chapter 8, "We are saved by hope." Hope is the experience of positive anticipation. It's challenging to live as Christ if we cannot ride in the saddle of hope since life moves to the left and the right and gives us ups and downs. If we don't have hope, we have no salvation because our strength is limited, and life's adversity destroys unstable faith. Unstable faith is what many Christians have, as they want to demand all life experiences to be positive. However, genuine faith means that regardless of life circumstances, I stay positive within the context of my being!

KEY VERSE

- *"If you faint on the day of adversity, your strength is small."* (Proverbs 24:10)

In the stages of our life where hope killers try to derail our positive experiences, we must remember the stories of suffering, pain, trauma, and other life experiences that true believers have endured because of hope.

Don't let your hope be destroyed, have faith, and be positive! Let your life be remade in Christ. As the Bible declared in Romans 8, we are saved by the joyous anticipation of a future in heaven, where we shall reign with Christ! My hope is not in this world or the people of this world. My hope is in Christ. Therefore, I enjoy the fellowship of those of you who have really found a life based on hope. Today, Christians endure real-life

experiences and maintain a hopeful perspective, and you will be saved and live happily!

PRE-THOUGHT:

My stability and joy come from Christ. My hope is in Jesus and His sacrifice on the cross. Therefore, I look forward to experiencing good today.

NOTES

PART III

INTENTION

THE
BOUNCE

THINK DELIBERATELY;
LIVE DELIGHTFULLY

A ccording to Dr. William Tiller, "For the last four hundred years, an unstated assumption of science is that human intention cannot affect what we call 'physical reality.' Our experimental research of the past decade shows that, in today's world and under the right conditions, this assumption is no longer correct. We, humans, are much more than we think we are, and Psychoenergetic Science continues to expand the proof of it." Psychoenergetic refers to the power or force of mental/spiritual activity. In short, what we feel and how we purpose our thoughts, words, and actions cannot affect physical human reality. [38]

Tiller believes that our intentions can impact our physical surroundings. He developed crystal-based silicon that can collect the intentions directed by people in meditation. Their collective intentions resonate at such a high frequency that they can be widely broadcast to affect other people. Tiller has used this technology to change the pH of water by one point on the pH scale, grow larvae 30% faster, and kill bacteria 30% more quickly. Through Tiller's research, we can see a

connection between our intentions and our physical surroundings. Science considers the spirit to be a proven side of self! [11]

THE PASTOR'S PERSPECTIVE

Given the content of Dr. Tiller's article and writings, I continue to be amazed at the ability of science to seemingly catch up to the word of God. A discussion of intent is essential to the believer who desires to be "effective" and is the centerpiece of living by faith. The above article demonstrates a scientific reference that shows that the mind of science is discovering that, as human beings, we have not only power but also authority to affect things around us by utilizing the energy that God has placed within us. This is a tremendous revelation that we, and seemingly the science community, finally understand what the word of God stated millennia ago.

KEY VERSE

- *"For the word of God is quick, and powerful, and sharper than any twoedged sword, piercing even to the dividing asunder of soul and spirit, and of the joints and marrow, and is a discerner of the thoughts and intents of the heart."* (Hebrews 4:12 KJV)

KEY DEFINITION

- *Intent - (intelligence, thought), intention, purpose.*

INTENTIONS: EARTH TO GOD

- *"If my people, which are called by my name, shall humble themselves, and pray, and seek my face, and turn from their wicked ways; then will I hear from heaven, and will forgive their sin, and will heal their land."* (2 Chronicles 7:14 KJV)

INTENTIONS: GOD TO MAN

- *"For the preaching of the cross is to them that perish foolishness; but unto us which are saved, it is the power of God. For it is written, I will destroy the wisdom of the wise and will bring to nothing the understanding of the prudent. Where is the wise? Where is the scribe? Where is the disputer of this world? Hath not God made foolish the wisdom of this world? For after that in the wisdom of God the world by wisdom knew not God, it pleased God by the foolishness of preaching to save them that believe."* (1 Corinthians 1:18-31 KJV)

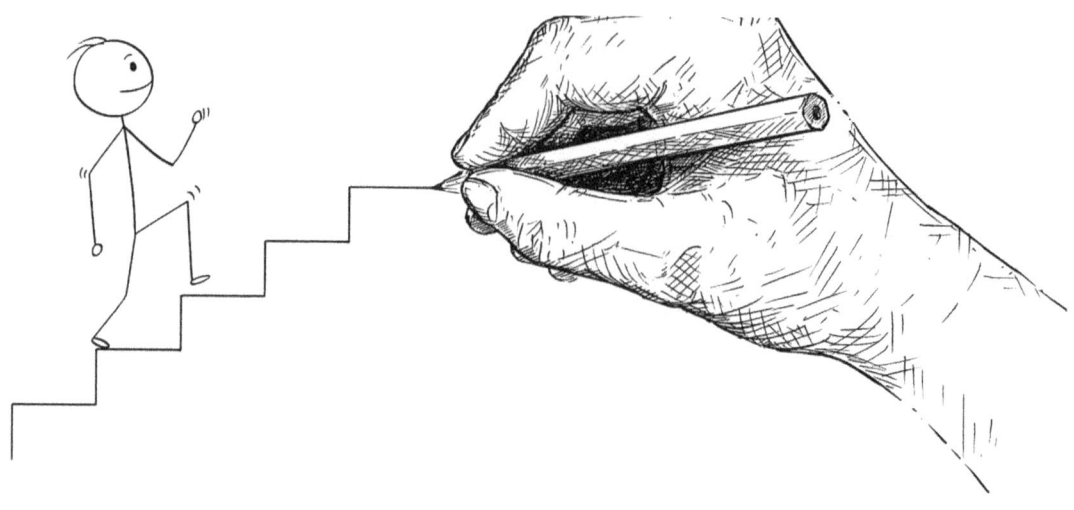

Intent is designed by God within the context of humanity to allow us to accomplish several important protocols if we want to make Heaven our home! To presume that the experience of being "born again" through baptism and the infilling of the Holy Ghost is all it takes for us to be Heaven-bound is irrational and self-serving.

Below are a few biblical references that relate to "intent." The first one, of course, is listed in Acts 10:29, which is a question Peter the apostle asked Cornelius at the birth of the Gentile church. The question is, "What is the intent." The meeting between Peter and Cornelius and his family was supernaturally determined through Peter having a trance and Cornelius having a vision. This vision and trance indicate that somewhere in the intangible "spirit realm," there was a Heavenly intention manifest through human interaction that created a salvation experience for all of those not fortunate enough to be the sons of Abraham.

- *"Therefore came I unto you without gainsaying, as soon as I was sent for: I ask therefore for what <u>intent</u> ye have sent for me?"* (Acts 10:29 KJV)

The second scriptural mention of intent that I've chosen comes from the book of Hebrews and essentially shows us our trouble. I think it defines one of the reasons that we have a real problem with good biblical preaching. We subjectively choose the things we want to obey and the things we disobey by somehow saying that "the preacher missed the interpretation of the scripture." Perhaps we're saying that "I don't want God to use a preacher to reveal the real motivation for what I do." The writer of Hebrews indicates that the word of God is a discerner of the intentions of the heart. A wife who says "I love you" to her husband as he leaves but intends to be angry and frustrated at him may have said the words, but "the heart's intention " is different from the words framed. The Bible says that love does not hold grudges and does not think evil, yet we can utter, "I love you," with no intention of being kind or generous with our affection. Do not fear; the word of God discerns what you meant, and that is where we are measured.

A frustrated believer can say, "Well, God has too high expectations for me," but I'm saying I have no intention of being Christian. Yeah, good preaching does provoke the evaluation of our evil intentions. Maybe that's one of the reasons we don't turn away at the rebuke of the word of God or change behaviors to align accurately with His expectations because we have no 'intention' of changing.

The word of God will reveal your heart's intentions! Say things you mean, and mean things that you say. Put action behind your words, and watch how intent changes the people and things around you. Then, your world will become a brighter place.

PRE-THOUGHT:

Anticipate that the Word of God, through good preaching, will cause correction, reproof, and instructions in being righteous.

NOTES

THE BOUNCE

THINK WITH PURPOSE; LIVE WITH FULFILLMENT

Intentionality is defined as the fact of being deliberate or purposive. Regarding philosophy, intentionality is defined as the quality of mental states directed toward some object or state of affairs. [20]

Many cultures have traditions about people who can heal the sick or injured without touching them or sometimes even being near them. This is known as Distance Healing Intention (DHI). Leonard Leibovici studied patients with bloodstream infections who were prayed for many years after they were diagnosed. The researchers wanted to know if DHI would work through time, not just physical space. Compared to the control group, who had received no prayer, the group who had received DHI had shorter hospital stays and were generally healthier. Dean Radin gathered studies on DHI and found that overall. At the same time, DHI is the cause of increased health may seem like an illogical conclusion. The simple fact that the effects exist is, in principle, enough to believe. [34]

THE PASTOR'S PERSPECTIVE

Albert Einstein had a phrase, "spooky stuff at a distance," to explain unexplainable things like energy between two unrelated particles or life force. However, what has boggled scientists for a long time is the power of Intercessory prayer and its unexplainable ability to heal. Science defines itself as the religion of man's mind, which man can take on a god-like quality. Indeed, man's mind created many modern devices like cell phones, plasma televisions, and light bulbs. Therefore, I'm not too quick to criticize the power of the scientific mind. Still, science has difficulty transitioning through the gulf of information, which proves that there is a greater force than ourselves, yet it works within us. We, as Christians, know that the force is God.

John 1 tells us that He came to live with us, and His name is Jesus Christ. He accomplished many "mind-boggling" feats while walking the earth and left behind for us a legacy that we can choose to utilize or not.

Intention - The power behind the words we use, the actions we show, and the expressions on our faces as we interact. The intention is to bind together what is within us and express it toward someone or something outside of us. According to scientists, it's 'spooky' how intention can affect objects and people around us.

KEY VERSE

- *"For the word of God is quick, and powerful, and sharper than any twoedged sword, piercing even to the dividing asunder of soul and spirit, and of the joints and marrow, and is a discerner of the thoughts and intents of the heart."* (Hebrews 4:12 KJV)

My hope is that today we can live with intention. Draw together all your thoughts, energy, motivation, and feelings to project love and acceptance toward other people. Realize that intentional living can comfort and uplift those around us. We can have a positive or a negative effect on those around us. We can build someone up or tear them down in a 'spooky' distanced manner. I will choose to pray for those around me that God will heal them and bless them. I'm going to start with myself. I intentionally move to my priority relationships, and ultimately, I will move to love my neighbor. Jesus understood that we have power! Jesus said In Acts 1:8,

- *"You shall receive power after that the Holy Ghost has come upon you, and you shall be witnesses"* (KJV)

Let your total self be a witness to the value of other people; and enjoy building something worthwhile in those around you today. Those good people around you will satisfy the longing for closeness within you.

PRE-THOUGHT:

By finding the positive impact situation's have on my life I am inspired to intentionally influence those around me in a positive way.

NOTES

THE BOUNCE

THINK AFFIRMATIONS

Within the context of Yoga, "Sankalpa" is the concept of daily affirmations that lead to the belief that if we know what we want and regularly articulate it, we can use "magic" to manifest those desires into our lives. Now, this is not really magic. It simply manipulates our mind's neuroplasticity or stretches it to believe differently. Psychiatrist Richard Davidson described how we're learning to shape our brains by changing our habits. The brain's neuroplasticity means that the brain can restructure itself to best solve the problem when we encounter new challenges. When we face the same challenge repeatedly, the neural pathways become smoother, and we solve the issues faster. Often, this occurs consciously, but we aren't aware of it most of the time. Davidson's team is researching the intentional training of the brain to improve well-being. Similarly, social psychologist Amy Cuddy has been studying how our body language affects our mind, specifically how pretending to be powerful can make your body feel more powerful. [41]

Dr. William Tiller's research team has used science to prove the effects of the mind on the matter that surrounds us. Specifically, they measured the change in electrical currents of objects exposed to intentional meditation. Tiller took four experienced meditators, each focused on an electrical device. That device was then sent to a lab 2000 miles away, where it was placed next to a water container. The goal was to either raise or lower the pH of the water by one whole unit simply by the proximity of the device and the intention of the meditation. Tiller's team measured a pH change of as much as 1½ units. Additionally, they discovered that the effect becomes permanent when an intentional meditation is repeated in one location. The pH change happened faster and in larger increments when the team repeated the experiment. Tiller said, "The alteration in the room's space has remained stable for well over a year, and it's still going strong." [37]

THE PASTOR'S PERSPECTIVE

KEY VERSE

- *"Blessed is the man that walketh not in the counsel of the ungodly, nor standeth in the way of sinners, nor sitteth in the seat of the scornful. But his delight is in the law of the Lord; and in his law doth he meditate day and night. And he shall be like a tree planted by the rivers of water, that bringeth forth his fruit in his season; his leaf also shall not wither; and whatsoever he doeth shall prosper. The ungodly are not so: but are like the chaff which the wind driveth away. Therefore the ungodly shall not stand in the judgment, nor sinners in the congregation of the righteous. For the Lord knoweth the way of the righteous: but the way of the ungodly shall perish."* (Psalm 1:1-6 KJV)
- *"Now unto him that is able to do exceeding abundantly above all that we ask or think, according to the power that worketh in us, Unto him be glory in the church by Christ Jesus throughout all ages, world without end. Amen."* (Ephesians 3:20-21 KJV)

In the article referenced above, science proved that today's intention is to create and reflect energy. Our meditations imprint the environment of our mind, body, and atmosphere of our home. If we focus on violent and evil thoughts, we create a hostile environment. We, literally, will create an energy that reflects these meditations. If we chose positive reviews, we would have a positive environment.

Some would say, "Well, I did not intend to think this way, but the other person caused me to be angry, seditious, evil speaking, less than loving, and not encouraging." Then, feel justified in not controlling their 'inner self.' I am sorry, but this excuse is lame and quite lazy. Let's be Christian and live scientifically. As a challenge, try controlling your personal space via intentional positive thinking. Immediately self-talk good things—don't wait another minute! Do not let one more negative intention settle in your brain, or it might slip out of your mouth.

Never forget that the way you intend to think is like a thermostat in your body and will affect the atmosphere in your room. Your intentions impact your environment and those around you. Make this your daily creed: "Today, I intend to love those close to me through word and action. I intend to accept all of those around me, even if they can hurt me. If my intention to help them is strong enough, I shall have an effect because of my intentions."

To be blunt, don't think insensitive and angry thoughts. They will only generate a stupefied, enraged environment around you and destroy the people that must endure your mind. Those types of thoughts hinder the joy, peace, and pleasure you will have throughout the day. According to the reference above, it may even change the pH of the water near you.

In John 7:38, Jesus reports, "He that believeth on me, as the scripture hath said, out of his belly shall flow rivers of living water." Our intention will determine the warmth of that flow.

PRE-THOUGHT:

I intend to positively warm those around me by keeping a positive, warm intention within me.

NOTES

THE BOUNCE

THOUGHT DISCIPLINE

Researchers at Stanford University studied endurance during exercise and feeling full while eating. The researchers tested participants for a gene that makes a person more or less prone to tiring. They were then asked to run on a treadmill before being randomly divided into two groups, with one group being told they had the gene and the other being told they did not. The participants were then asked to run on the treadmill again. Those who were told they had the tiring gene didn't run as long as they had before, while those who were told they had the better endurance gene ran longer than they had in the first part of the study. This occurred regardless of the actual genetic results. [40]

THE PASTOR'S PERSPECTIVE

It seems that in the world of human existence through the lens of Christianity, there are naturally two groups of people. The first group has been born into a world known to be fallen, and where they only hear dark things. In this dark world, people are predators, abusers, destructive, go about carnally, and have the capability of hurting each other. This darkness comes very naturally and doesn't need any kind of advanced teaching, according to Isaiah 60:1-2.

KEY VERSE

- *"Arise, shine; for thy light is come, and the glory of the Lord is risen upon thee. For, behold, the darkness shall cover the earth, and gross darkness the people: but the Lord shall arise upon thee, and his glory shall be seen upon thee."* (Isaiah 60:1-2 KJV)

This dark world is a place where flesh rules, and it is every man or every woman for themselves. This pursuit of carnality shows that no one is safe from potential harm.

In the dark world of carnality, people attempt to dispose of the proof of their choices and actions. We get married and ruin the relationship through the pursuit of selfishness. Then, we try to cover the evidence of it through a divorce. When we become physically intimate with a member of the opposite gender, a seed begins growing, and we hide reality through abortion. We are the victims of other people's terrible treatment. We try to cover the proof held clearly, within our memory, by becoming dependent on artificial synthetics like alcohol or drugs. We are victimized in childhood by bullies, and we become wrath-filled and belligerent to try to conceal that we feel vulnerable.

In the book of Galatians, chapter 5, the works of the flesh are described as adultery, fornication, wrath, strife, sedition, heresy, envy, murder, drunkenness, and revellings. This happens when people have only heard that you have the carnal gene and were 'born that way.' A second group on the earth has had the advantage of having heard that they don't have to live according to the rules of darkness. They don't have to abuse one another, and they don't have to seek only what is good for themselves. This group is the body of Christ! We, who are part of his Church, are so fortunate! When we come out of the waters of baptism after repenting, we begin to 'hear' that we have new genes (we have a new father). In the way we used to live our lives, we were destroyers, but now we come into the body of Christ. Then suddenly, "Faith comes by hearing and hearing by the word of God," and we recognize the sound of new life. When we get on the treadmill of existence, we suddenly have more endurance, less capacity for sin, and more desire to build the people around us.

The first group has no hope because all they hear is the world's entertainment, music, and stories of despair and pandemics. However, in the second study group, the body of Christ, we have learned to conform to a world that is not a part of the darkness. Our Lord empowered us when He said, "You are the light of the world" (Matthew 5:14). Also, the Lord said, "Nothing shall be impossible to you" (Matthew 17:20).

According to the study of human nature, you will become what you've heard you can be. You actually believe the report of the things you're listening to and the words you're hearing. Then, the sad continuation of this reality is that I have made the people around me become what I have said they are. How about we develop the body image of heaven by becoming loving, peace-giving, seeking satisfaction for other people, serving one another with love, and creating within our own sphere of influence a reality that is the result of "the preaching of the cross." The single most significant moment in all of eternity was when Jesus Christ made it all the way to the cross without sin, so we could hear that we've got an opportunity to choose a new dad, our father in heaven, who gives me the genes of love.

PRE-THOUGHT:

I am the world's light, and the darkness has no hold on me. Therefore, I will think light toward all men.

NOTES

THE BOUNCE

MELODY OF INTENTION

The power of intent can be seen in some parts of Africa, where mothers write and sing songs for their children while they are pregnant. Then, when the mother is not within earshot of their crying child, they sense the child's distress and sing the song. The child, in return, senses the mother's song and calms themselves. This is true even in business. If a CEO or manager asks for feedback from their team but does not really plan to use it, the team will not be honest. Most people can easily perceive the intentions of those around them. [26]

Einstein once observed what he called "spooky action at a distance." More modern research on physics has named this concept: entanglement and non-locality. In physics, entanglement occurs when two particles are so wholly connected that they cannot be affected separately, even if they are not anywhere near each other. We can see this phenomenon outside of science in our relationships. For example, if you suddenly think about a friend you haven't seen in a while, then they call you, that's quantum entanglement. Similarly, twins often know what the other is thinking or feeling. This phenomenon has been known in society as "twin telepathy" but is likely another example of quantum entanglement. [11]

Modern science has assumed that human intention has no effect on reality. Dr. William Tiller's research shows the exact opposite. His team is discovering how "we humans are much more than we think we are," and Psychoenergetic Science continues to expand the proof of it. [38]

THE PASTOR'S PERSPECTIVE

You are at this point in your life exactly where you have thought yourself to be!

According to Harvard Business School and Albert Einstein, intent provides influence even from a distance!

KEY VERSE

- *Unto me, who am less than the least of all saints, is this grace given, that I should preach among the Gentiles the unsearchable riches of Christ; and to make all men see what is the fellowship of the mystery, which from the beginning of the world hath been hid in God, who created all things by Jesus Christ: to the intent that now unto the principalities and powers in heavenly places might be known by the church the manifold wisdom of God, according to the eternal purpose which He purposed in Christ Jesus our Lord: in whom we have boldness and access with confidence by the faith of him. Wherefore I desire that ye faint not at my tribulations for you, which is your glory. For this cause, I bow my knees unto the Father of our Lord Jesus Christ, of whom the whole family in heaven and earth is named, that he would grant you, according to the riches of His glory, to be strengthened with might by His Spirit in the inner man; that Christ may dwell in your hearts by faith; that ye, being rooted and grounded in love, may be able to comprehend*

with all saints what is the breadth, and length, and depth, and height; and to know the love of Christ, which passeth knowledge, that ye might be filled with all the fulness of God. Now unto him that is able to do exceeding abundantly above all that we ask or think, according to the power that worketh in us, unto him be glory in the church by Christ Jesus throughout all ages, world without end. [Amen.] (Ephesians 3:8-21 KJV)

- *"Jesus answered and said unto them, Verily I say unto you, If ye have faith, (intention) and doubt not, ye shall not only do this which is done to the fig tree, but also if ye shall say unto this mountain, Be thou removed, and be thou cast into the sea; it shall be done. And all things, whatsoever ye shall ask in prayer, believing, ye shall receive."* (Matthew 21:21-22 KJV)

Paul wrote about the power of intent long before the scientists understood that it was even subject matter to be considered. Paul preached with intention, and the church can hear and, by reflection, implement the strategies (powerful intent) of our Creator through obedience to biblical mandates.

The research cited above shows that the right intention can create and grow a business. Moreover, a mother who intends to please her child can do so, even from a distance, beyond the physical ability of the child to hear her voice, just because she intends to comfort the baby. What if we took the science of intent and couple that with the intention of the word of God?

Obedience to the principles of God's Word allows the intention of a God who seems so far away to become the reality of where we live, within close confinement of other human beings around us.

Consider the effect that this could have on:

1. Your spouse - What if we intended to ensure that our spouse was equipped with the highest level of loving intent? What if I really focused on my feelings of love for and for my spouse today? According to science, I can provide my spouse with comfort and unconditional support even from a distance. Could this be why the apostle Paul said, "Husbands love your wife and wives submit yourselves to your husband[s]?" (Ephesians 2:22). Unless we "intend" to give it a spin, we'll never know. Our marriages are precisely where we thought they would be. Do you want your spouse to be more successful? Then, through the power of intention, believe that it's happening, and it will happen.

2. Your children - Taking to heart the description of what happens in the African community, where the mother intends to soothe her child by conditioning the child's mind within the context of a particular song written with intention by a loving mother. Could it be that our children are exactly where their parents have nurtured them to be both in the world and in Christ? Their ability to learn, implement, strategize for life, engage others in relationships, and rise to the challenge that being a Christian requires of them to reflect our intention as a parent. Perhaps, that's why in the book of Deuteronomy, the Word tells us to teach these principles daily and place them like front lights between the eyes and as a signet on our hands.

3. The church culture - What if I stopped judging other people according to my insecurities and interpreting their values by how they appear on the outside? Could it be that if my intention is to love my brothers and sisters, my love will, even from a distance, affect how the church culture grows? I have a responsibility to keep a clean heart, have a ready mind, and pour into my brothers and sisters. Mark my words, it will all be sorted out when you stand in that white throne room, and your actions and words will bring judgment, not to you targeted, but rather the target your words and actions have painted on your own soul as seen in Matthew 7:1-2.

4. The world around us- I am literally commanded to have good intentions toward myself and my neighbors. Jesus thought that all the law and the prophets should hang on to one idea. To love God with all my heart, soul, mind, and strength, and I would love my neighbor as I love myself. It is a tragedy for those who can't love themselves enough to reach someone outside our puny little circle and extend love. We may deserve judgement and could receive it at the hands of our own inactivity and unwillingness to teach anyone around us about the love of God that should be within us. We are whited sepulchres, beautiful outside but dead inside. We are unknowingly preparing ourselves for an eternity away from the God who intended for us to be so much more in this world.

How many of us have cursed the fig tree of our life? Our judgment and condemnation of others have come back to our own lives and are raining the fruit of our own vine. Jesus said faith was released, and what was become of the fig tree was a fruitless death to the roots (Matthew 21:19-22). Many of us have done this to our own marriages and our own children. By not sharing the Word with those

around you, you've allowed your neighbors to continue to live in darkness, all because you intended to do that very thing!

What hope do those around us have if the power within us intends to do nothing? If my intention is to do nothing, the results shall be seen. Right now, without hesitation, decide to intentionally affect your own mind by thinking positive thoughts about what you can become. Make it your intention to be what He has called you to be, a tree of love, peace, joy, temperance, long-suffering, goodness, and faithfulness.

Right now, with intention, ask God to bless those around you and perhaps even repent for how you have influenced people up to this point in your life. Call out to God for His mercy, and He will hear you and allow you the opportunity to have a second chance at love. Let's stop ruining people and allow the Lord to build us into the temple He's called us to be. A beautiful place where love is not only shown but where love through intention is released into a dark world so desperately needs this light. Thus, be the solution God wants you to be.

PRE-THOUGHT:

I will prepare to make a difference by becoming the difference I want to make. Love improves all things, and I will use it generously.

NOTES

THE BOUNCE

CHOOSE GOOD INTENTION; LIVE GOOD RELATIONSHIPS

Richard Gordon believes most modern scientists do not look at psychic phenomena because they believe the world functions mechanically. However, Gordon has gathered multiple studies that show the mind's impact. Gordon discussed Dr. Tiller's study on DHI raising the pH of water. Dean Radin performed an analysis and found that a person observing photons traveling through slits can affect the photon's path. Lynn McTaggart performed an experiment where 10,000 people from 80 countries focused their mental energy on influencing a single leaf to glow brighter than a leaf that received no attention. [17]

Earl Nightingale developed the concept of what he called "The Strangest Secret." The secret is why some people are successful while others are not. According to Nightingale, only 5% of men at age 65 have achieved the financial success they had hoped for. However, do 95% of people really fail at their goals? To find the answer, Nightingale defined success as "the progressive realization of a worthy ideal." Therefore, success is relative to each individual person. Success does not have to be financial; it simply does whatever job you've always wanted. Nightingale says that so many people 'fail' because they conform to society and act like everyone else without discovering themselves. The one concept that all wise thinkers through history agree on is that: we become what we think most. [28]

THE PASTOR'S PERSPECTIVE

For each of us our personal happiness, satisfaction with life, all of our marriage and parenting experiences, our business life, cash flow, and acquired assets are all a very telling story read by all. The investment of our time and experiences we have had have all been meticulously authored by the thoughts that each of us have allowed into our mind and which have ultimately become who we are!

KEY VERSE

- *"Blessed is the man that walketh not in the counsel [principles of thought] of the ungodly, nor standeth in the way of sinners, [those adhering to Adamic indulgence of rebellion to the Words of God] nor sitteth in the seat of the scornful. [Embittered mockers of life in Christ] But his delight is in the law of the Lord; and in his law doth he meditate day and night. And he shall be like a tree planted by the rivers of water, that bringeth forth his fruit in his season; his leaf also shall not wither; and whatsoever he doeth shall prosper. The ungodly are not so: but are like the chaff which the wind driveth away. Therefore, the ungodly shall not stand in the judgment, nor sinners in the congregation of the righteous. For the Lord knoweth the way of the righteous: but the way of the ungodly shall perish."* (Psalm 1:1-6 KJV)

As typical of science, if you dig deep enough, you see that many of their experiments are deliberately set in motion by the Lord God Almighty to confirm His word. In the investigation, "A Focused Intent," the designer of the test chose two leaves. One of the leaves was the target of people worldwide, thinking positively that the leaf would "glow." In the controlled environment of that experiment, the leaf that was considered positively indeed "glowed much brighter" than the leaf that was ignored.

The prophetic power of David was that the example written in Psalm one indicates that if we meditate on God's law (intention), we receive all of the positive thoughts of heaven. We become the leaf (life) that eternity chose to ignite glowing power on this earth. Think of the concepts of our Lord as related through the authors of the gospels: "If you love me keep my Commandments" (established thought), "You are the light of the world" (glowing influence) (John 14:15, Matthew 5:14). In other words, you are the glowing leaf who demonstrates the focus thoughts of heaven that we will shine. Think of the prophet Isaiah, "Arise and shine for the latest come, and the glory of the Lord is risen upon Thee" (Isaiah 60:1).

My personal choice is to disengage from negative thoughts. To disengage from the belief that if I think negatively, I will receive a positive. I'm going to choose, instead, today to think about the word of God and what it reveals to me. I'm thankful that the Word revealed that I was a sinner, so I could genuinely repent of my sin! I'm glad that revealed to me a path was laid for me, starting with the precious stone laid in Zion. That a name wherein I could be baptized for the remission of sin was given to me. I am also thankful that it was shown to me that I could receive the power of the Holy Ghost with the evidence of heaven's speaking through me, the tongues of men and angels! I'm also thankful that it didn't leave me as a newborn babe but gave me an opportunity for daily and eternal instruction in what heaven determined is righteousness.

The truth is that your marriage is what you thought it would be, your children will grow to be exactly as you think they should, your finances are precisely what you want, and your friendships on earth are just as valuable as you've made them. Hey, word to the wise on this beautiful day, stop being unrealistic, negative, and the sole determiner of your own misery.

Take the apostles as an example. Rise and walk in a new life with Christ. Be a glowing leaf. Start thinking about something you want to become and watch how your thoughts usher you into that new reality. Not because science is so bad, but because long before scientists ever discovered this idea, the word of God had established it from the foundation of the world. His name is Jesus, by the way!

In the words of Gerry Goffin and Carole King, "Will you still love me tomorrow?" Hopefully, you will hear the melody of love as you pursue "leaf!" Get it, pursue "leaf?" Pursue life thinking positive thoughts. Glow and become what you've always wanted to be. I believe you can do it!

PRE-THOUGHT:

I am at least 50% responsible for each relationship that I have. I choose therefore to add 100% of the warmth needed to make these relationships amazing.

NOTES

THE BOUNCE

THINK STRENGTH;
LIVE STRONG

Brian Clark and his colleagues wanted to test the brain's impact on strength development. They designed a study where, for four weeks, 14 people had a cast put on their arm that immobilized their wrist and hand. Fifteen additional people did not have casts. The ones who had the cast were asked to perform mental imagery exercises five times a week to imagine that they were moving the immobilized wrist. The other 14 did no exercises. After the four weeks, the group who did not perform the exercises had 45% less strength than the control group. The group who completed the exercises had 25% less strength. Clark believes that this study shows the impact our brain alone can have on our physical body. The experiment results demonstrate that when they thought right, even without physical exercise, the participants maintained strength. [3]

THE PASTOR'S PERSPECTIVE

Strength in the Bible. It is mentioned most in Psalms 70, Isaiah 33, and Job 22. Strength is mentioned in 39 books and occurs 232 times in the Bible.

KEY VERSE

- *"For this cause I bow my knees unto the Father of our Lord Jesus Christ, Of whom the whole family in heaven and earth is named, That he would grant you, according to the riches of his glory, to be strengthened with might by his Spirit in the inner man; That Christ may dwell in your hearts by faith; that ye, being rooted and grounded in love, May be able to comprehend with all saints what is the breadth, and length, and depth, and height; And to know the love of Christ, which passeth knowledge, that ye might be filled with all the fullness of God. Now unto him, that can do exceeding abundantly above all that we ask or think, according to the power that worketh in us, Unto him be glory in the church by Christ Jesus throughout all ages, world without end. Amen."* (Ephesians 3:14-21 KJV)

In the verse above, Paul indicates that strength is something fostered within us. He begins this writing in the posture of a "bended knee," which means prayer and meditation on God. We are to be "strengthened" with might by His spirit in the inner man.

Fear, jealousy, and envy are all spiritual immobilizers. These stem from a core belief that something terrible will happen in the inner man. When fear hits us, we tend to recoil and not do anything. Then we meditate on how scary life is and consequently do nothing. In a way, we are in a "lifecast" where we do nothing. We then complain that we have nothing.

The solution to this mental sickness is to stop letting fear immobilize your love. Begin to use your imagination, think positively through this immobilization, and watch how God establishes steps for you. It's not the will of God that you would remain motionless or in an effortless place because you're afraid to move. Think of all the good that will come into your life if you release the strength of the inner person where the Spirit of the living God resides! Just thinking right will cause you to maintain the strength you didn't even know you had.

Whatever part of your life is gripped by fear, and needs to improve, just begin to think positive thoughts. Then, watch how God establishes a brand-new day for you! Marriages, parenting, and friendships can all be blessed if we imagine those relationships as healthy and prosperous. Remember what David said in Psalm 1, "But his delight is in the law of the Lord and in his law does he meditate both day and night. He shall be like a tree planted by the water. Everything he does shall prosper" (KJV).

Meditation is mental imaging, and we let that imaging focus on the law of God. We will bring the prosperity of heaven into our earthly life. I guess I could say that your relationships are stronger than you imagined. In the same case, your finances are more powerful than you imagined! Right now, imagine yourself being happier, and you will be more in love with your spouse. You will be a more effective, powerful parent. All of this is possible because just by thinking strength into your person. Think right, and you will experience strength!

Mold the way you feel by realizing personal strength is real.

NOTES

THE BOUNCE

INTENTIONAL MEDITATION; PERSONAL SATISFACTION

Mindful meditation can be an important tool for our mental health. Gaëlle Desbordes' research uses fMRI (functional magnetic resonance imaging), which scans the brain by taking and recording pictures. Specifically, Desbordes' 2012 research showed that people who meditate have more continuous brain activity than those who don't meditate. Desbordes scanned participants while doing everyday tasks, before and after meditation, for over two months. The scans detected slight changes in activity in the amygdala, the part of the brain associated with emotion. Previously, no activity changes were recorded in the amygdala. Desbordes' more recent research also uses fMRI technology to scan the brains of clinically depressed patients while they practice mindful meditation and again. At the same time, they ruminated on a series of phrases such as "I am such a loser" or "I can't go on." After a couple minutes, the patients were asked to stop ruminating, and the researchers measured how quickly the patients' brains disengaged from negative phrases. In the 1970s, professor Herbert Benson developed "The Relaxation Response" as the commonality between meditation, yoga, and religious prayer. Benson described this response as the opposite of the "fight or flight" response. [33]

THE PASTOR'S PERSPECTIVE

Are you repeating self-chatter using phrases like: 'I am such a loser,' 'I can't go on,' 'my kids are frustrating,' 'I need to leave my marriage,' 'my job is my problem,' 'my spouse is my problem,' or 'my friends are my problem'? According to science, these are phrases used by people who are clinically depressed. It could be that you are repeating and chattering with those negative self-phrases because you are your problem. More specifically, the way we think is our problem. If this is you, do not make any major decisions right now. Do not make any massive life changes because you will regret them. Let me restate this, so I'm transparent with you. If you make a significant life decision while depressed without getting help, you will regret it when your mind finally comes back to normal.

KEY VERSES

- *"And God saw that the wickedness of man was great in the earth, and that every imagination of the thoughts of his heart was only evil continually."* (Genesis 6:5 KJV)
- *"And be not conformed to this world: but be ye transformed by the renewing of your mind, that ye may prove what is that good, and acceptable, and perfect, will of God."* (Romans 12:2 KJV)
- *"For to be carnally minded is death; but to be spiritually minded is life and peace."* (Romans 8:6 KJV)
- *"For who hath known the mind of the Lord, that he may instruct him? But we have the mind of Christ."* (1 Corinthians 2:16 KJV)
- *"In whom the god of this world hath blinded the minds of them which believe not, lest the light of the glorious gospel of Christ, who is the image of God, should shine unto them."* (2 Corinthians 4:4 KJV)
- *"Casting down imaginations, and every high thing that exalteth itself against the knowledge of God, and bringing into captivity every thought to the obedience of Christ;"* (2 Corinthians 10:5 KJV)

- *"But I fear, lest by any means, as the serpent beguiled Eve through his subtilty, so your minds should be corrupted from the simplicity that is in Christ."* (2 Corinthians 11:3 KJV)
- *"And be renewed in the spirit of your mind;"* (Ephesians 4:23 KJV)
- *"And you, that were sometime alienated and enemies in your mind by wicked works, yet now hath he reconciled."* (Colossians 1:21 KJV)

The beauty of science is that it constantly confirms what God's Word has stated for thousands of years. God has plans for us, and if we live the patterns of His book, The Bible, we will enjoy the results of his plans. He is an architect/master builder trying to help you build a life worth living. In the article above, the facts science discloses about the brain demonstrate the word of God. If we can learn to think and meditate on the word of God, our meditation will cause a change in the literal substance of our brain. Why spend a lifetime struggling with depression and anxiety when it is as easy as allowing the word of your Creator to show you how to change your thoughts. To not allow the word of God to change your life, you must be either unwilling (a rebellion), or you are unable, which would require that you cannot understand what I'm writing.

He has a beautiful life for you, free of addiction, anger, and destructive relationship patterns, so heed the word of God. Obey what comes forth from that word in the form of preaching. It's not about finding happiness. Living for the idea of happiness leads to walking in the counsel of the ungodly, allowing the way with sinners, and not allowing ourselves to sit in the seat of the bitter.

Now take a moment, and begin thinking about your closest human relationship, whether it is a spouse, a child, or if you are utterly alone in this world, just a relationship with yourself. Think happy and loving thoughts about that person we have identified. Hold onto those warm, loving thoughts, and watch how your brain will begin to think such thoughts about everything in your day. I don't need a yoga instructor or any therapeutic intervention if I allow myself to start to focus on the word of God and meditate on it all through the day and at night. Perhaps this will work for you too, but you'll never know until you try. I believe in you, and I believe in the power of God, His Word, and its ability to change the way we think. I hope that we can all reach a place of mindfulness and intentionality that pleases the Lord and gives us the greatest and happiest human experience while we walk this earth.

PRE-THOUGHT:

Since I will become what I focus on, I choose to meditate on a joyful breakthrough.

NOTES

PART IV

HATRED

THE BOUNCE

OVERVIEW OF HATRED

Psychologist Allison Abrams reviewed numerous studies and gathered the main forces behind why we hate: fear of self, fear of others, and lack of self-compassion; it fills a void of societal and cultural factors. Psychologist Patrick Wanis believes that hatred can be caused by love for things that we know and relate to or by aggression toward things that are different or seen as a threat. Psychologist Dana Harron argues that hatred can manifest from our fears of something inside of ourselves and that we then project that fear onto another person or object. Freud explained projection as the rejection of what we don't like about ourselves. Psychologist Bernard Golden believes that hating a group of people is simply a way to avoid finding our own identity and that we have to be taught to hate others. Hatred is not a natural response to things. Psychologist Brad Reedy believes we desire to be good, so we project our own "badness" onto something else that we can attack because we are afraid that our bad traits will cause other people to reject us and end up alone. [2]

Therefore, we typically hate simply due to the fear of different things. The best way to avoid hate is compassion for others and ourselves. If we genuinely accept every part of ourselves, we won't judge others. [2]

THE PASTOR'S PERSPECTIVE

Understanding the efforts of hatred is an integral part of the building blocks of truly Christian life. A life that provides each believer the opportunity to enjoy co-existing with others while we walk through our human experience. We will examine critical scriptural references found in the writings of Solomon, and many other scriptures defining and confining hatred, to expose any of its long-lasting effects that might reach any of us.

Acknowledging that hatred is possible in humans may motivate us to rid ourselves of this destructive process. Acknowledging that not only is God capable of hate, but He manifests it toward individuals will help us understand why we need to rid ourselves of this emotional plague. It would be great to be free of hatred toward yourself and others before you stand before God in His throne room of judgment. I look forward to discussing the changes He can make within each of us through dispelling hatred and, consequently, within the confines of a happier church; this will provide a happier you. Hopefully, we can learn to love others as we love ourselves. Living on this earth with hatred, variance, or even the slightest dislike for other human beings while here wastes your time and could also put you in the lake of fire for all of eternity. Consider these personal traits and these verses in mind as we begin our study.

KEY VERSE

• *"These six things doth the Lord hate: yea, seven are an abomination unto him: A proud look, a lying tongue, and hands that shed innocent blood, An heart that deviseth wicked imaginations, feet that be swift in running to mischief, A false witness that speaketh lies, and he that soweth discord among brethren." (Proverbs 6:16-19 KJV)*

KJV DICTIONARY DEFINITION FOR HATE:

HATE

Transitive Verb. To dislike greatly; to have a great aversion to. It expresses less than abhor, detest, and abominate unless pronounced with a peculiar emphasis.

IN SCRIPTURE. IT MEANS TO LOVE LESS.

HATE: Noun. Great dislike or aversion; hatred.

HATED: Past Participle. Greatly disliked.

HATEFUL: Adjective, Odious; exciting great dislike, aversion, or disgust. Example: All sin is hateful in the sight of God and of good men. That feels hatred, malignant, malevolent.

HATEFULNESS: Noun. Odiousness; is the quality of being hateful or of exciting aversion or disgust.

HATING: Verb. Disliking extremely; entertaining a great aversion for.

PRE-THOUGHT:

If I invest my energy in hatred, I miss out on the joy of connecting with others. I choose to nurture positive thoughts to create my best life!

NOTES

THE BOUNCE

EMPHASIS ON "A PROUD LOOK."

Pride has two primary meanings. The first is "A feeling that you respect yourself and deserve to be respected by others." The other is "A feeling that you are more important or better than other people." The first definition is a healthy aspect of pride necessary for good self-esteem, while the second causes excessive

pride in oneself. We need healthy pride to have stability in how much we value ourselves as individuals, regardless of our achievements. Those with an overinflated sense of pride often repel those around them since they can't see others as equally valuable as themselves. These people are typically overcompensating for a lack of self-pride. Pride can even prevent us from seeing our wrongdoings. Rather than being filled with an overinflated sense of pride, we need to have dignity in ourselves and others as human beings. [4]

Joan Cyril Abello lays out eleven signs of an overinflated sense of pride that you can use to evaluate yourself. Pay attention to the motivations behind what you are doing and thinking.

1. You think you are humble.
2. You do not accept constructive criticisms.
3. You always want to be the center of attention.
4. You are vain about your physical appearance.
5. You do not like associating with the "ordinary" or unpopular.
6. You are fond of name-dropping.
7. You are not teachable.
8. You do not listen to others' advice.
9. You are critical of those who have the potential to do better than you.
10. You think you are too important to do mundane things.
11. You do not like to be surpassed by anyone. [1]

THE PASTOR'S PERSPECTIVE

The six things the Lord hates begin with the concept of a "proud look." Since all things in The Word have deeper meanings, we understand that there is an external and internal meaning to all concepts discussed in the canonized scripture. As Solomon describes the building blocks of becoming a biblical abomination, keep this in mind. We should pay close attention to how we are given a picture of things we don't want to be.

Remember, the idea of a proud look through the context given above means having low self-esteem on the inside but wanting to appear high, super important, and better than other people on the outside. This means when you look inside, through the eyes of man and the world, you see very little; so when you look outside, you have to try to act really big. Truly scripture defined this distorted look like the beginning of an unfruitful life, which leads to a destructive end.

In Deuteronomy chapter 6, Moses tries to help us understand a great concept of God and the importance of loving Him with all of our heart, soul, and strength. If we could adopt this positive pattern in our life, we would not have trouble loving and caring for the people around us. When we don't have a great sense of ourselves, seeing ourselves through the eyes of God, there is no way to have a proper sense of seeing the value in others. This is one of the effects of being conceited. Since we have nothing really to offer on the inside, we sure can judge everybody around us.

Never forget, our God is an architect, and Solomon shows us how the things we truly do not want to build into our lives. Pride can be defined as the epitome of laziness. If I have low self-worth, there is very little hope that we will engage other people by serving them.

KEY VERSES

- *"When pride cometh, then cometh shame: but with the lowly is wisdom."* (Proverbs 11:2 KJV)
- *"The fear of the Lord is to hate evil: pride, and arrogancy, and the evil way, and the froward mouth, do I hate."* (Proverbs 8:13 KJV)
- *"Be of the same mind one toward another. Mind not high things, but condescend to men of low estate. Be not wise in your own conceits."* (Romans 12:16 KJV)
- *"A man's pride shall bring him low: but honour shall uphold the humble in spirit."* (Proverbs 29:23 KJV)
- *"But the Lord said unto Samuel, Look not on his countenance, or on the height of his stature; because I have refused him: for the Lord seeth not as man seeth; for man looketh on the outward appearance, but the Lord looketh on the heart."* (1 Samuel 16:7 KJV)
- *"But he that glorieth, let him glory in the Lord. For not he that commendeth himself is approved, but whom the Lord commendeth."* (2 Corinthians 10:17-18 KJV)
- *"Before destruction the heart of man is haughty, and before honour is humility."* (Proverbs 18:12 KJV)
- *"And he said, That which cometh out of the man, that defileth the man. For from within, out of the heart of men, proceed evil thoughts, adulteries, fornications, murders, Thefts, covetousness, wickedness, deceit, lasciviousness, an evil eye, blasphemy, pride, foolishness: All these evil things come from within, and defile the man."* (Mark 7:20-23 KJV)

Let's kick pride to the curb! Let's begin to serve the Lord through studying His word and thinking the right thoughts about other people. Practice being humble by doing the things that humility calls us to do. First, begin with the Lord by proclaiming his Lordship over our lives. Then, let this humility become the drawing power of God that others see in you. Allowing this change to happen in you means that you don't have to be correct or superior; you can rejoice with those who rejoice because humility causes you to weep with those who weep.

Begin with your closest earthly relationship, whether that is a spouse or other meaningful and life-giving connection. Enter that relationship today with humility, and show the other person how valuable they are by showing through humility how valuable God sees you.

PRE-THOUGHT:

A proud look can create distance between me and others. I choose to embrace humility and connect with genuine appreciation for those around me.

NOTES

THE
BOUNCE

EMPHASIS ON
"A LYING TONGUE."

As we consider the following list of things that the culture sees as lying it becomes clear why the Lord hates a lying tongue. Jesus described himself as "the way, the truth, and the life." Anything less than that is living below the blessings that he has called us to live within. These blessings are available when we live within the confines of "truth!" This list is lengthy but not all encompassing.

- A lie is a false statement that is used to deceive others. Different types of lies can be used for many various reasons.
- A bare-faced lie is clearly incorrect information to the hearer.
- A big lie is a lie of considerable magnitude.
- A blue lie is done for the greater good.
- A bluff is a lie that one has something they genuinely do not have.
- B.S. is a lie that the speaker may not even believe themselves but is said to give the hearer a specific impression.
- A cover-up is used to hide a previous lie or action.
- Defamation is a lie that hurts the reputation of someone else.
- Deflecting is avoiding the subject of the lie.
- Disinformation is intentionally spreading false information.

- An exaggeration is a lie where most of the statement is true, but only up to a certain point.
- Fake News is lies spread by the news media outlets.
- A fib is a lie that is easy to forgive.
- Fraud is a lie used for financial gain.
- A half-truth only has part of the truth.
- Jocose lies are understood within the group to be teasing and humorous.
- A lie-to-children occurs when we oversimplify what we tell children.
- Lying by omission is when most truth is told, but critical facts are left out.
- Lying in trade is when a company advertises false information about its products.
- A memory hole is a lie where a person edits documents or photos to remove something from existence.
- Minimization is a lie where aspects are toned down to deny them.
- Mutual deceit is a lie wanted by both the speaker and the hearer.
- A noble lie is told to maintain law and order.
- Pathological lying is consistent and compulsive behavior.
- Perjury occurs when a person lies while under oath in court or in an official sworn statement.
- A polite lie may be needed depending on the culture of the speaker or hearer.
- Puffery is an exaggerated claim that cannot be proven false.
- Speaking with a forked tongue means that a person is hypocritical in what they say and do.
- Lastly, a white lie is seen as harmless by the speaker. [44] How many kinds of lies have you told?

THE PASTOR'S PERSPECTIVE

KEY VERSES
- *"But the fearful, and unbelieving, and the abominable, and murderers, and whoremongers, and sorcerers, and idolaters, and all liars, shall have their part in the lake which burneth with fire and brimstone: which is the second death"* (Revelation 21:8 KJV)

- *"Keep thy tongue from evil, and thy lips from speaking guile."* (Psalms 34:13 KJV)
- *"Lying lips are abomination to the Lord: but they that deal truly are his delight."* (Proverbs 12:22 KJV)
- *"Lie not one to another, seeing that ye have put off the old man with his deeds; And have put on the new man, which is renewed in knowledge after the image of him that created him."* (Colossians 3:9-10 KJV)

- *"Ye are of your father the devil, and the lusts of your father ye will do. He was a murderer from the beginning, and abode not in the truth, because there is no truth in him. When he speaketh a lie, he speaketh of his own: for he is a liar, and the father of it."* (John 8:44 KJV)

Lying is procreative, meaning that lying once leads to other lies. We see that lying had a father as we have read the scriptural premise in John chapter 8. The procreator of all liars is defined by scripture as "Satan." Psychologists have popularized the statement, "all people lie." I believe this to be misleading; it would be more accurate if it stated, "All people have lied."

The prophet Isaiah, in his writings of chapter 28, states to humankind, "Because ye have said, We have made a covenant with death, and with Hell are we at agreement." This statement implies we as the human species have found agreement with the teaching of, the lifestyle of, and a covenant with darkness, the place where all liars will spend eternity.

God hates pride and a lying tongue. The tongue has such great power as it can speak to give life or death. The list of the types of lying above is very humorous to me. Since the book of Revelation says, "All liars have their place on the lake of fire," meaning all lies are death statements that smack the face of the Life-Giver. While the scriptures also say many other sins guarantee you will be put in the eternal abyss, a place where the fire is not quenched, and those sweet tiny worms never die. I find it interesting that it can be paraphrased as "all types of lies, and those who speak them, are having an affair with Satan." Consequently, those who tell the truth by using their lips honestly have an honest relationship with heaven! Truth tellers are courting the path that leads to the place where Jesus is forever and ever.

God hates liars because they are inappropriately affectionate with a father of lies and, by doing so, have sealed their eternal fate. However, lying is not the only death we cause with our tongues. Backbiting means speaking negatively about anyone who is not there to defend themselves. A backbiter is openly engaging in the accustional, procreative nature of destruction. Participating in negative verbal behavior will bring you, through the destructive power of these lies, to an eternal place far from love, joy, and peace and put you on a bed of worms in the lake of fire. It is a  sobering but necessary one! We are to seriously think about what we say and focus on giving life with our tongue, not causing death! You should only desire to tell the truth about Jesus and how He loves all people. Think about those things, so you can speak about those things.

One of the most truthful things we can do is repent of our sins! The vocalization of realizing that our soul was bound by darkness because of our improper actions and attitudes allows us to speak the truth that will cause Heaven to rejoice! The language of repentance is literally vocalizing before God that you recognize your affair with Satan has brought you into the place where you broke the heart of your eternal love, the groom, named Jesus! Take a minute right now and repent before God and decide right now to never return to those lies. When you rise from that place of repentance, recognize not only does heaven rejoice, but you can embrace people with a tongue that will speak of life!

PRE-THOUGHT:

A lying tongue can erode trust and damage relationships. I choose to speak with honesty and integrity, knowing that truth builds stronger connections.

NOTES

THE BOUNCE

EMPHASIS ON "HANDS THAT SHED INNOCENT BLOOD."

Human beings kill their own species more viciously than any other mammal group. Maria Gomez and her team studied the amount of lethal violence from 1,024 different species of mammals. They found that 0.3 percent of animal deaths occur from their own species. However, with humans, that rate increases to 2.3 percent. R. Douglas Fields, Ph.D., believes this difference could partially stem from our intense desire to defend ourselves and our belongings from others outside of our social group. Males are measurably more violent than females. Violence is an innate aspect of humanity. [13]

In 2008 Colin Pritchard and Tony Sayer from Bournemouth University published their survey of child homicides in England occurring over ten years. They found that children under five are most likely to be attacked by their own family members. This survey highlights the difference between intra-familial and extra-familial killers. Pritchard and Sayer did not find a single case of a child under five having been attacked by someone outside their family.

In the majority of cases, the assailant was the victim's parent, typically the mother, who was suffering from a mental disorder. In all the cases where the father was the assailant, they ended their own lives after their child died. [31]

THE PASTOR'S PERSPECTIVE

Proverbs 6:17 asserts God hates "hands that shed innocent blood." This can be defined as human extremities that pour out the blood of innocent animals in a slaughter-like fashion and kill others within our species. The concept of innocent blood really relates to being "guilt-free." Indicating that three categories of victims would mean (1) very young children, (2) animals that kill only for food and sustenance, and (3) those reborn in Christ. The reborn have had an authentic, new birth experience through repentance, the remission of sins in baptism in Jesus's Name, have felt the infill of the Holy Ghost, and have risen to walk in the newness of life! With this definition in mind, the human species kills innocence and is a murderer.

KJV DICTIONARY DEFINITION: MURDER

MURDER, noun.

1. The act of unlawfully killing a human being with deliberate malice by a person of sound mind. To constitute murder in law, the person killing another must be of sound mind or in possession of his reason. The act must be done with malice prepense, aforethought or premeditated. Still, malice may be implied, as well as expressed.
2. An outcry when life is in danger. MUR'DER, verb.
3. To kill a human being with premeditated malice. See the Noun.
4. To destroy; to put an end to. MURDERER, noun.
5. A person in possession of his reason unlawfully kills a human being with premeditated malice.
6. Consisting in murder; done with murder; bloody; cruel; as murderous rapine.
7. Bloody; sanguinary; committing murder; as murderous tyranny.
8. Premeditating murder; as murderous intent or design.

KEY VERSES

- *For this is the message that ye heard from the beginning, that we should love one another. Not as Cain, who was of that wicked one, and slew his brother. And wherefore slew he him? Because his own works were evil, and his brother's righteous. Marvel not, my brethren, if the world hate you. We know that we have passed from death unto life, because we love the brethren. He that loveth not his brother abideth in death. Whosoever hateth his brother is a murderer: and ye know that no murderer hath eternal life abiding in him. Hereby perceive we the love of God, because he laid down his life for us: and we ought to lay down our lives for the brethren. But whoso hath this world's good, and seeth his brother have need, and shutteth up his bowels of compassion from him, how dwelleth the love of God in him? My little children, let us not love in word, neither in tongue; but in deed and in truth. (John 1:1-18 KJV)*

The biblical definition of brother is "a member of your religious community," which has nothing to do with a natural bloodline but with the bloodline of Christ, as received in baptism in Jesus' name! "Agape" means love, which is defined as never between the genders, but how Christ loved us and gave His life for us. As it says in verse 15, If you see a brother with a need and do not give to that brother, you are likened to a murderer. Wowser! This means when I am not letting God's love flow through me to the members of the body of Christ, I have defined myself as a hater and a murderer. A pretty high standard was given by the apostle John. If loving a brother or a sister in Christ is difficult for you, Jesus will overlook your vanity, bitterness, gossip, backbiting, lack of providing for the needs of others, and the sheer willingness to let people go without because you hold the ability to flow with love. One of the most remarkable powers provided through the Holy Ghost is the ability to love my neighbor. Therefore, I can be a witness and no longer a murderer. However, according to the world's excuse, it is in your natural DNA that murder is acceptable, and hatred is normal. We're entertained by murder; we're drawn to it, like a mysterious magnet reaching down inside a natural propensity to kill.

Those we kill most often are the people of God. Who He died to redeem, and who are washed in the innocent blood of a Savior who successfully navigated a sinful world without sin.

In summary, if love is not flowing through me to the members of the body of Christ, I might as well not plan on spending an eternity in heaven. All that remains without the flow of love is the natural man, who is tribal, territorial, and easily triggered to murder those who "threaten our little paradigm." Take a broader picture. If I'm not loving my neighbor, I have not really learned to love myself. I can not see myself through the eyes of my crucified creator God. He hung on the cross to redeem my neighbor and me. It is a tragedy if I have been filled with the power of the Holy Ghost and cannot find the strength to walk across the territory of my yard to extend a loving gesture to those right next to my domain.

Aren't you glad, Christian, that you are a lover of people? Today is your opportunity to demonstrate to heaven that you're a vessel that He can flow through because you're willing to love not only Him but also your spouse, children, and grandchildren. You will flow into your neighborhood with the power of light. Come on, let's grow the body of Christ by loving the unloved. I don't want to be part of the hands that call out innocent blood to be shed and poured out for no reason!

PRE-THOUGHT:

Since I am called to convey love, I must be mindful of what my hands touch and the actions I take.

NOTES

EMPHASIS ON "AN HEART THAT DEVISETH WICKED IMAGINATIONS" (SORROWFUL TROUBLE)

Sadness is an emotional response to specific adverse events that every person will experience occasionally. It typically does not last more than a few days and leaves after a person experiences a joyous occasion. The best treatments for sadness are expressing it and time. Depression, on the other hand, is an overwhelming sadness that has no specific reason behind it. The best treatment for depression is a combination of medication and therapy. [16]

Dr. Vikaas Sohal and his group of researchers have discovered a possible link between depression and anxiety and overactive communication between the two sides of the brain. When measuring the electrical activity in the brain, they found an increased level of activity in the memory and emotion areas when a person is sad. This clearly shows that our mood has an effect on our brain. Sohal and his team found that, overall, a negative attitude occurs with an increase in the electrical communication between the amygdala, which processes emotions, and the hippocampus, which processes memories. Sohal believes that this is physical proof of a relationship between negative memories and negative emotions. We still do not know the exact relationship between memories and emotions or which part of the brain starts the chain. Still, now we know that a biological relationship between the two exists, which will significantly aid future research. [36]

THE PASTOR'S PERSPECTIVE

Hearts that devise "wicked" imaginations are one of the fundamental building blocks in becoming an abomination in the eyes of God. Wicked imagining involves what Solomon declares as:

KEY DEFINITIONS

- Wicked - Troubling or Sorrowful.
- Imaginations - Flights of man, evading deep thoughts of God.
- Deviseth - Continuing to make connections.

We could summarize this portion of Proverbs as one of the building blocks to becoming an abomination in continuing to have deeply troubling and sorrowful thoughts and making connections of those thoughts to the people around us.

Why would God hate this sort of thinking? Why would perpetual sadness and its connection to human beings put us in jeopardy of losing out with God?

KEY VERSES:

- *"And the Lord, he it is that doth go before thee; he will be with thee, he will not fail thee, neither forsake thee: fear not, neither be dismayed."* (Deuteronomy 31:8 KJV)
- *"The righteous cry, and the Lord heareth, and delivereth them out of all their troubles. The Lord is nigh unto them that are of a broken heart; and saveth such as be of a contrite spirit."* (Psalm 34:17-18 KJV)
- *"Blessed are they that mourn: for they shall be comforted."* (Matthew 5:4 KJV)
- *"Casting all your care upon him; for he careth for you."* (1 Peter 5:7 KJV)
- *"For his anger endureth but a moment; in his favour is life: weeping may endure for a night, but joy cometh in the morning."* (Psalm 30:5 KJV)

Christians must realize when they meet Jesus that they are "born again." God, as the Creator, understands that life brings sorrow and pain. However, when we meet Him, we have become "a new creature." The Lord says, within the context of being a new creature, "All things have become new." All things mean everything, including our heart, soul, mind, and physical strength. If I allow my heart to continue connecting negative emotions in historical opinion to current people, I judge them by my historical paradigm. Therefore, I am continuing in my sadness, which means I have literally no joy and strength. The power of God does not create anemic, sad, angry, or bitter people. It creates new creatures that walk with joy and peace and have found happiness!

The experience of the new birth is all-encompassing. When we follow His instructions and "meditate on the Lord day and night," we will delight in serving God through submission and love. We are just human beings meandering through the sorrow of life, continually reminded of how people have failed us and how sad we are to be alive.

The Bible says, "What fellowship does Christ have with an unbeliever." This verse indicates that we will not be the same person as unbelievers once we have become Christian. When we are following the Lord through His Word, the darkness that used to make us sad and the memories of personal pain and loss from what people have done to us can no longer move through us to affect those around us. Being perpetually sad after meeting Jesus is a step toward becoming an abomination. It robs the Lord of the opportunity for us to love our neighbors since our heart connects sadness to the people around us.

Sadness robs us of evangelistic zeal and the desire to introduce other people to Jesus, who corrected all of our sadness! If the Jesus I serve was not strong enough to give me happiness in today's experiences, why would I ever introduce anyone else to Him? It's like a person who has faith, but no works will continue to walk in the lust of the eyes, the lust of the flesh, and the pride of life. Therefore, they will never be able to have those good and happy thoughts or feelings since they have not connected activity to their beliefs. These believers will remain sad, unusable, and even dangerous to the people closest to them.

The Lord doesn't hate you if you are a person who struggles with a dower outlook or is continually judging people because you don't feel good about yourself, but He does hate that pathology! When He said, "Come out from among them and be separate saith the Lord," He wants us to include the verse, "We should come away from our own thoughts and let this mind be in you which was also in Christ Jesus." It would be terrible going through life sad, then to be sent away from God because we were ineffective witnesses.

Will you let Him now wipe away your tears and let the word of God heal your sorrow? Meditate on that question today instead of the memories that hurt so deeply. Begin to have a new thought process about life as you see sinners through your own eyes of forgiveness and your ability to carry a cross. This start will make a difference. Let the joy of the Lord fill your heart and become what He has called you to be! Remember, you are awesome in the eyes of God!

PRE-THOUGHT:

I will create no space for wickedness in my imagination, allowing room for positive thoughts that inspire right actions.

NOTES

THE BOUNCE

EMPHASIS ON "FEET THAT BE SWIFT IN RUNNING TO MISCHIEF."

Greed has existed in humanity since the beginning. When used well, it is the driving force behind progress. However, greed can also cause economic misery in a culture run by materialism. There are seven main warning signs of greed in a person. The first is being self-centered with no regard for others. Second, having intense envy for what others have. Third, having no care for how their actions affect others' feelings. Fourth, wanting more than what they have. Fifth, they easily manipulate others to their will. Sixth, they want immediate results for their greed. Seventh, they have no regard for morals and ethics in cheating their way to their goal. The hard part for those affected by someone else's greed is waiting for them to change.

The greedy person has to notice their faults and desire to change for themselves. This can be difficult because of how greed affects their view of themselves and others. It is our job to guide them once they need it. [21]

THE PASTOR'S PERSPECTIVE

Feet that are swift and running to mischief! In Strong's dictionary, this phrase means that the sole of the foot is set in the greediest direction to scatter and idolatrize the destruction of pastureland while murdering others and emphasizing lustful self-satisfaction. Whew, sounds like everybody else. Not me, right? It would be great if I could just stop now and not be defined or break down the terrible, consequential choice to mindlessly follow the culture we live in now.

KEY VERSE

- *"And Saul was consenting unto his death. And at that time, there was a great persecution against the church which was at Jerusalem; and they were all scattered abroad throughout the regions of Judaea and Samaria, except the apostles. And devout men carried Stephen to his burial, and made great lamentation over him. As for Saul, he made havoc of the church, entering into every house, and haling men and women committed them to prison."* (Acts 8:1-3 KJV)

Through the persecution of Jesus Christ by the Jews, the Church at Jerusalem was born. Political leaders and religious leaders not only plotted but consented and advocated for the death of the one truly innocent man who ever lived, Jesus Christ. They quickly, and under the cloak of night, judged, pummeled, beat, and led Him away to be crucified. That was where we crucified innocence, love, and concern only for others. The cross demonstrates the utter and complete yielding of the sole of humanity's feet, growling and without compunction. Murdering and celebrating the death of deliverance from evil, hope for humanity, and the greatest love we would ever see demonstrated.

We learn from Jesus' sacrifice and Acts, Chapter 2, about the church's birth. First, coming to the lost children of Israel with the great apostle. Then, Peter delivers the message that corrects our behavior to quickly pursue mischief. In Acts chapter 8, before the birth of what is the Gentile church, we see there is the apostle who was not consenting to the death of the innocent Christ. Now the greedy crowd has their soles set to pursue the death of an innocent Stephan without compunction! Our great apostle Paul "consented" to the end of the innocent martyr. Jesus Christ, whose blood washes the pillar of the Church of God, moved beyond the children of Israel and into the backyard of my humanity.

This brings us to the concept in Proverbs chapter 6 that you and I as gentiles must overcome the propensity to swiftly, greedily run toward the idea that "I am saved, and others are lost." Then, I consent to the culture of death to murder my neighbor, fellow workers, or others while I religiously sit in the safety of His love and refuse to love others. I'm greedy for my own salvation but deny it to those around me. They could be innocent of His death too if they were only given the opportunity to repent. I don't want to be trapped by Satan. To have only the great motivation to see myself saved while becoming greedy as I consent by religiously judgmental silence to the rest of the world being sent to a dark place. Motivation, complete loss, and the pursuit of murder are not only about taking pleasure in others' rise destroyed, but means I am so greedy in the search for my own loss I consent to the murder of this group of beautiful, hopeful people. These are people bound by the sin, which my testimony and encouragement could literally revoke from the

The choice to be a sinner comes very naturally to the human species, but let's not be like the unconverted Saul of Tarsus. Saul, before being reborn, was determined to destroy the body of Christ through religious judgment. That Saul consented to the death of innocence, such as Stephen, who was stoned (Acts 7:54-59). Jesus provided the greatest opportunity to self-judge when He said, "Let him without sin cast the first stone." Christians can become so trapped in the greed and desire to be saved that the soles of our feet are motivated by a lust for salvation. We consent to our neighbor's death through silence when we are so greedy. but as Romans chapter 1:32 says, "Who knowing the judgment of God, that they which commit such things are worthy of death, not only do the same but have pleasure in them that do them." People who have accepted Jesus know better but choose not to be better. Therefore, they decide to live in the culture of death, darkness, the pursuit of lust and stay lost in sin.

Whew, am I ever glad that I am not like the others lost in sin. Remember what we have studied this day and consider this verse as we keep our walk with God.

KEY VERSE

- *"And he spake this parable unto certain which trusted in themselves that they were righteous, and despised others: Two men went up into the temple to pray; the one a Pharisee, and the other a publican. The Pharisee stood and prayed thus with himself, God, I thank thee, that I am not as other men are, extortioners, unjust, adulterers, or even as this publican. I fast twice in the week, I give tithes of all that I possess. And the publican, standing afar off, would not lift up so much as his eyes unto heaven, but smote upon his breast, saying, God be merciful to me a sinner. I tell you, this man went down to his house justified rather than the other: for every one that exalteth himself shall be abased; and he that humbleth himself shall be exalted."* (Luke 18:9-14 KJV)

PRE-THOUGHT:

I will choose to walk the path of integrity, avoiding the temptation to rush into mischief.

NOTES

THE BOUNCE

EMPHASIS ON "A FALSE WITNESS THAT SPEAKETH LIES."

False accusations are untrue claims of wrongdoing. There are three main types of false accusations. The first is an entirely false allegation. Second, an assertion describes events, but the accused person is innocent. Third, an allegation is false but mixes in descriptions of events. False accusations can be either intentional or accidental for any number of reasons. [43]

People often form intense opinions about others with a single piece of information. When those opinions are negative, it can lead to false accusations. Defending oneself against false accusations can be likened to torture due to emotional and mental strain on the person. Freud believed that this internal emotional pain is the worst kind of human experience. [7]

THE PASTOR'S PERSPECTIVE

Proverbs 6:19, in the context of our study, means an injurious falsehood spoken in a court of law with exuberance and excitable passion, a human pretentious false prophecy! Before moving to the list of verses for today's study, please take a moment to read Jesus's words in Matthew chapter 7:1, "Judge not!" Now, take a moment to consider these other verses:

- *"Thou shalt not bear false witness against thy neighbor."* (Exodus 20:16 KJV)
  - o *"Thou shalt not bear false witness"* forbids: Speaking falsely in any matter, lying, equivocating, and in any way devising and designing to deceive our neighbor. Or speaking unjustly against our neighbor, to the prejudice of his reputation.
- *"These six things doth the Lord hate: yea, seven are an abomination unto him: A proud look, a lying tongue, and hands that shed innocent blood, An heart that deviseth wicked imaginations, feet that be swift in running to mischief, A false witness that speaketh lies, and he that soweth discord among brethren."* (Proverbs 6:16-19 KJV)
- *"A false witness shall not be unpunished, and he that speaketh lies shall not escape."* (Proverbs 19:5 KJV)
- *"A false witness shall not be unpunished, and he that speaketh lies shall perish."* (Proverbs 19:9 KJV)
- *"Wherefore putting away lying, speak every man truth with his neighbour: for we are members one of another."* (Ephesians 4:25 KJV)
- *"But the fearful, and unbelieving, and the abominable, and murderers, and whoremongers, and sorcerers, and idolaters, and all liars, shall have their part in the lake which burneth with fire and brimstone: which is the second death."* (Revelation 21:8 KJV)

These three witnesses of how our God looks at false information include the law of Moses, the wisdom of Solomon, in the words of God manifest in the flesh. We should probably take note of this concept and determine that we will not be guilty of this. When considering the psychology of accusation, we would have to note another person's perception and what motivates their actions. However, it is literally impossible for any other individual to be solely determined by our judgment or know precisely what caused a person to act in any particular way. The judgmental Christian is guilty of assuming what the word of God leaves in its own authority or God's destined role of His child. A judgmental Christian is guilty of assuming the role of what the Word of God leaves in it's own authority "dividing asunder between soul and spirit and as a discerner of the thoughts and the intentions of the heart" (Hebrews 4:12). The nature of false accusation is something that belongs only to the judge and is punishable by eternity away from God. For that reason, Moses said not to do it, Solomon said God hates it, and Jesus said, "In the same way you judge others, you will be judged" (Matthew 7:2)!

There are two instances in Proverbs 6 display building blocks to becoming an abomination before God related to lying. The first one is that God hates a lying tongue. The second one says that God hates "a false witness that speaketh lies." The first reference is accurately paraphrased: anyone who lies is in jeopardy of being hated by God, much like Esau (Malachi 1:3). The second instance relates to the "court of law" by using the word "witness." This would indicate that instead of lying about stuff you've been doing, you are trying to vehemently and with great passion publicly accuse someone of being permanently guilty.

Being judgmental is like calling someone who gives you an angry look "a hater" or someone who looks at another person with improper sexual motivations as being forever guilty of cheating or being an adulterer. Although the haters and the adulterers are to face eternal punishment, the word of God says those on the accusation side or the judgment side will also face separation from God. Does that seem unfair? It makes sense when you look at how the Lord Jehovah God wants us to live a full life of peace and happiness. When I waste mental energy by engaging in negative thought processes, accusing, or judging others, even those I believe are guilty, all I do is rob myself of the three tenants of Christian living: love, joy, and peace.

We can be so consumed, mentally, by the wrongs of others that we become a victim of our own rampaging wrath. A Christian may not ever voice condemnation, but holding onto resentment and pridefully looking down at someone for mistakes real or assumed, is wrong.

As Christians, we are called to be peaceful, loving, and engaging with others in a bond of peace. Let the cross and the beautiful Savior who was hung on it judge what others intended to do or actually did. Let us just think well of all people and live fully with outright joy and fervor, so we can lead others to the cross. Do not view others as unforgiven sinners; see them as pre-forgiven individuals who will see what the power of forgiveness and repentance offers them and others. Sounds like a joyful way to live, the way God intended for us to live!

PRE-THOUGHT:

Truth is balanced and serves as a firm foundation. I will not bear false witness, as it is an abomination.

NOTES

THE BOUNCE

EMPHASIS ON "HE THAT SOWETH DISCORD AMONG BRETHREN."

People with a high-conflict personality tend to blame others for their own problems because they don't realize or want to realize they are the cause. People with high- conflict personalities have four basic traits: consistent targets of their blame, all-or-nothing thinking, unmanaged emotions, and extreme behaviors. They may also have characteristics indicative of five different personality disorders. The first disorder is antisocial disorder. These are not people who "just don't feel like hanging out," but they do combine charm with cruelty to reach their goals. The second disorder is a narcissistic personality disorder. These people have fragile and inflated self-esteem while constantly putting down those who are "below" them. The third disorder is borderline personality disorder. These people cling to those close to them and lash out at any slight or perceived abandonment. The fourth disorder is a paranoid personality disorder. These people are very suspicious of those around them because they believe that others are only there to attack them. The last disorder is a histrionic personality disorder. These people seek constant attention and tend to cause drama with their exaggerated stories. However, not every person with these disorders has a high-conflict personality. If they do not have consistent targets for their blame, they do not have a high-conflict personality. [12]

THE PASTOR'S PERSPECTIVE

KEY VERSES

- *"For lack of wood the fire goes out, And where there is no whisperer, contention quiets down."* (Proverbs 26:20 NASB)
- *"For you are still fleshly. For since there is jealousy and strife among you, are you not fleshly, and are you not walking like mere men?"* (1 Corinthians 3:3 NASB)
- *"Therefore the Jews were grumbling about Him, because He said, "I am the bread that came down out of heaven."* (John 6:41-43 NASB)
- *They were saying, "Is not this Jesus, the son of Joseph, whose father and mother we know? How does He now say, 'I have come down out of heaven'?" Jesus answered and said to them, "Do not grumble among yourselves."* (John 6:34 NASB)
- *"Now I urge you, brethren, keep your eye on those who cause dissensions and hindrances contrary to the teaching which you learned, and turn away from them."* (Romans 16:17 NASB)
- *"Remind them of these things, and solemnly charge them in the presence of God not to wrangle about words, which is useless and leads to the ruin of the hearers."* (2 Timothy 2:14 NASB)
- *"As I urged you upon my departure for Macedonia, remain on at Ephesus so that you may instruct certain men not to teach strange doctrines, nor to pay attention to myths and endless genealogies, which give rise to mere speculation rather than furthering the administration of God which is by faith."* (1 Timothy 1:3-4 NASB)

- *"Keeping away from strife is an honor for a man, But any fool will quarrel."* (Proverbs 20:3 NASB)
- *"Make friends quickly with your opponent at law while you are with him on the way so that your opponent may not hand you over to the judge, and the judge to the officer, and you be thrown into prison."* (Matthew 5:25 NASB)

The church's inception is recorded in Acts chapter 2 as happening after "they were all in one place and in one accord," indicating everybody was getting along and everyone had pulled together to form an alliance. That alliance was then blessed by God's new and dynamic presence in the church. Suddenly, there came a sound from heaven when the people got along. The Lord of glory poured out His Spirit immediately and ushered in what is now "the church age."

This church age will end with something called "the rapture." This is an excellent catching away of what He defines as "the body of Christ" or "the bride without spot or wrinkle!" If you pursue the scripture further, it says that God adds to the church when the body of Christ has favor with God and with man. Assuming we can all learn to get along, we can all be prepared to go up in His heavenly presence. Sometimes people with high-conflict personality disorders refuse to rein in every thought to the obedience of Christ, and they go about verbally spewing all of the toxins which have been put into their thinking through childhood trauma and improper examples they have witnessed.

The danger of allowing your high conflict personality disorder to manifest within the group of people whom the Lord has redeemed is that God hates it. "Well, you don't understand, Pastor; I just don't always feel good about people." The truth is God hates it because He loves the people our words divide us from. Other excuses are; 'I'm just a gossip' 'They we're looking at me funny or when i am troubled by something I just have to talk with someone about it'' God hates it!

Those are examples of the six things the Lord hates and seven which are an abomination unto Him. We ruin our reputation because we perceive some falsehood. We decide to ruin our personal relationships by continuing and blaming others for the terrible self-esteem we are allowed to linger because we refuse to learn, behave or trust others. In John 3, Jesus indicates that to be a part of the bride of Christ, and be pulled out of this world when He returns, we must "be born again of water and spirit." Being reborn gives us a brand-new Father, God, and hope that we can accept others. Therefore, why allow these building blocks to be an abomination unto God?

This one is the most troubling to a Pastor of all of these. This is where the group can grow, but because of one personality disorder, many can be hurt as well. Stop allowing yourself to think improperly about other people. Remember the key verse from Matthew 7. Judging others will be the gateway to eternal separation from God for many of those people. Thus, when you come into the church, check your high-conflict personality at the door or desire to love unconditionally! Before walking in, accept that you must stop judging everybody according to the disorder of your thoughts.

PRE-THOUGHT:

Unity is essential for harmony. I will choose to promote peace and sing a song of togetherness.

NOTES

_____

_____

_____

_____

_____

_____

_____

_____

_____

_____

_____

_____

_____

_____

_____

_____

_____

_____

PART V

WORDS

THE
BOUNCE

COMMUNICATING VERBALLY

Time magazine released an article where Rev. Franklin Loehr, a chemist trained at Illinois Monmouth college, turned Presbyterian minister, conducted a test where two rows of seeds were planted from the same package. All received the same amount of watering and care, but one row was cursed by a woman, and the other row was prayed for. The results of this experiment were shocking as 100% of the seeds that were prayed over flourished and brought forth fruit, but all of the seeds that were cursed by the woman, save one, became twisted and distorted with no fruit evident, and they died. The research team looked to Mark 11:20, where Christ cursed a fig tree, and in a matter of hours, it was "dried up from the roots." [39]

THE PASTOR'S PERSPECTIVE

The continuous fight science has with Christianity, and God's Word is an immense struggle for what is called faith. The scriptures declare "the tongue has the power of life or death" (Proverbs 18:21 NIV), and the experiment above

provides a great picture of this truth being enacted by a scientist. The proof of the death grip of words is much more prevalent in our culture.

How many homes have been destroyed by death, divorce, hate, accusations of infidelity, or what Solomon referred to as the contentious words of a wife? How many single people don't self-speak love, acceptance, and the power to grow? There are countless children who have been victimized by harsh parental communication demeaning their intelligence and value! Take control of your life today by taking control of your words! Let the root, the seed, and the fruit of who you are in Christ become a display to the world of all that is good and lovely!

Your life as an individual human being has the seed power to become a mighty nation or a light in a darkened world. If you're married, your marriage is like a seed planted in the ground, and the fruit of our marriage is like the sampling study of the scientist referenced above! If we let the seeds receive negative words and cursing, we will have the fruit of that. Love can and does die every day; that's why the Lord our God said, "Man cannot live by bread only but by every word which proceeds out of the mouth of God" (Luke 4:4).

I want to let my words give life today, so when I wake up in the morning, I greet the Lord with a hearty welcome into my life. I next speak words of encouragement to myself as a husband and father. I will speak to my wife, words of love and affirmation, speak to my children, words of hope, and declare life. To those I am fortunate enough to mentor, I will speak words of hope and courage in a culture trying to make us fear and isolate ourselves!

Come on, Christian. Speak ginormous words of love and life today, and watch a "newness" come into your circle of love! Be the power of blessing and stop the flow of cursing. This is the most extraordinary power we will ever know! I'm on your side.

PRE-THOUGHT:

If I choose my words wisely, I will avoid appearing foolish.

NOTES

THE BOUNCE

STOP NEGATIVE COMMUNICATION

The Trump administration does not allow the CDC to use seven specific words: evidence-based, science-based, vulnerable, fetus, transgender, diversity, or entitlement while proposing budget funds. When publicly announced by The Washington Post, the public health and policy communities were in an uproar. Oregon Democratic Senator Jeff Merkley tweeted, 'Are you kidding me?!?!' The American Public Health  Association wrote 'This. Is. Unacceptable.' Does it really matter if certain language is avoided in official documents sent to government agencies? Scientific American interviewed Lera Boroditsky, a cognitive scientist, about what happens when we use certain words and not others in our daily life or in our work? According to Boroditsky, words have power. Saying that a hamburger is 80 percent lean or 20 percent fat is essentially communicating the same thing. But people perceive the 80 percent lean hamburger as healthier than the 20 percent fat hamburger. You can choose how others think about something by framing and talking about it specifically. [24]

THE PASTOR'S PERSPECTIVE

Here, the lesson is to stop letting words that kill out of our mouths. Why would I continue to speak poorly toward others when God's Word and scientific data suggest that words have power?

SOLOMON

- *"A man's belly shall be satisfied with the fruit of his mouth; and with the increase of his lips shall he be filled. Death and life are in the power of the tongue: and they that love it shall eat the fruit thereof. Whoso findeth a wife findeth a good thing, and obtaineth favour of the LORD. The poor useth intreaties; but the rich answereth roughly. A man that hath friends must shew himself friendly: and there is a friend that sticketh closer than a brother."* (Proverbs 18:20-24 KJV)
- Principle- Words determine direction.

ISAIAH

- *"I have seen his ways, and will heal him: I will lead him also, and restore comforts unto him and to his mourners. I create the fruit of the lips; Peace, peace to him that is far off, and to him that is near, saith the Lord; and I will heal him. But the wicked are like the troubled sea, when it cannot rest, whose waters cast up mire and dirt. There is no peace, saith, my God, to the wicked."* (Isaiah 57:18-21 KJV)
- Principle- What you speak, He creates

THE APOSTLE PETER

- *"Likewise, ye wives, be in subjection to your own husbands; that, if any obey not the word, they also may without the word be won by the conversation of the wives; While they behold your chaste conversation coupled with fear. Whose adorning let it not be that outward adorning of plaiting the hair, and of wearing of gold, or of putting on of apparel; But let it be the hidden man of the heart, in that which is not corruptible, even the ornament of a meek and quiet spirit, which is in the sight of God of great price."* (1 Peter 3:1-4 KJV)
- Principle- The female gender has word authority in relationships. Not only does this pertain to marriage, but also to who we are as the bride of Christ. We influence heaven by the words we use on earth. Peter says to wives, your words within the context of your marital relationship are more potent in the hearing of your husband than the words that proceed out of the mouth of God.

The very idea that we have a right and can choose to speak about people, institutions, leadership, or church culture in any way that we 'feel' speaks not only about our ignorance as humans but also clears a path for us to spend an eternity without God. The politicians of the day react harshly when threatened with the loss of specific terms from their shared vocabulary. They realize that if you replace specific terms. Then, you correct misappropriated thought. They absolutely recognize the scientific fact that you shape opinion by your words.

What would happen within the body of Christ if we took heed to how we talk to other people and about other people regarding the exceptional individuals that make up the 'church'? A brother to a brother? A sister to a sister? A parent to child? A husband to a wife? A wife to a husband? A teacher to students? Students to their teachers?

Perhaps if we are lonely, we could recognize that we likely have no friends because our language is death. Our marriage is dissatisfying because our language is death. Our finances struggle because our language is death. We are not content with who He created us to be because we speak death. Take advantage of your social standing to lock yourself in with a positive mind. Think well, begin to speak well, and start to live well. It is scientifically based that people judge you by the words you use, but the Word of God indicates we judge ourselves by the words we use.

I have said so many times, friend, you are exactly where you thought you would be at this moment. As we have studied this concept, we see that your life reflects the words you alone have used. He has definitely created the fruit of your lips. Be glad that our God never fails to give us life or death according to our words.

PRE-THOUGHT:

Negative speaking damages relationships; therefore, I will choose to speak positively to nurture great connections.

NOTES

THE

BOUNCE

CHOOSE WORDS CAREFULLY

The words you choose in your mind become reality because reality is subjective. This truth causes problems when your mind is consistently negative. However, you can change this by using positive self-talk to reshape how you see your situations. This "top-down" processing is how the various parts of your brain work together. Your prefrontal cortex is the "up brain," while your subconscious is the "down brain." The prefrontal cortex sends directions and messages to the  subconscious, forming and storing memories. Making your brain think only positive self-talk can make you see the world more optimistically. Psychologist Gary Lupyan says, "Perceptual systems do the best with inherently ambiguous inputs by putting them in context of what we know and expect. Studies like this are helping us show that language is a powerful tool for shaping perceptual systems, acting as a top-down signal to perceptual processes. In the case of vision, what we consciously perceive seems to be deeply shaped by our knowledge and expectations." A simple "yes" or "no" can also significantly impact our perceptions. Simply thinking "yes" can tell our brain to go ahead. However, thinking "no" can tell our brain to stop. Mary Kay said, "If you think you can, you can. If you think you can't, you're right." [8]

THE PASTOR'S PERSPECTIVE

The above is a great article that demonstrates that the truth written about in the word of God concerning faith (confidence) is played out in everyday life by those who do not profess to know Christ.

KEY VERSE

- *Now faith is the substance of things hoped for, the evidence of things not seen. For by it the elders obtained a good report. Through faith we understand that the worlds were framed by the word of God, so that things which are seen were not made of things which do appear. By faith Abel offered unto God a more excellent sacrifice than Cain, by which he obtained witness that he was righteous, God testifying of his gifts: and by it he being dead yet speaketh. By faith Enoch was translated that he should not see death; and was not found, because God had translated him: for before his translation he had this testimony, that he pleased God. But without faith it is impossible to please him: for he that cometh to God must believe that he is, and that he is a rewarder of them that diligently seek him. (Hebrews 11:1-6 KJV)*
- *Be careful for nothing; but in every thing by prayer and supplication with thanksgiving let your requests be made known unto God. And the peace of God, which passeth all understanding, shall keep your hearts and minds through Christ Jesus. Finally, brethren, whatsoever things are true, whatsoever things are honest, whatsoever things are just, whatsoever things are pure, whatsoever things are lovely, whatsoever things are of good report; if there be any virtue, and if there be any praise, think on these things. Those things, which ye have both learned, and received, and heard, and seen in me, do: and the God of peace shall be with you. (Philippians 4:6-9 KJV)*
- *"Let the words of my mouth, and the meditation of my heart, be acceptable in thy sight, O LORD, my strength, and my redeemer." (Psalms 19:14 KJV)*

When the psychological community outside of God confirms what the word of God has boldly declared for thousands of years, it stands to reason that we would listen and do what these two declare.

Therefore, speak something positive to yourself, someone close to you, or someone you want to draw near you again. Words can bring healing or inflame anger. The choice is all up to you.

Incredibly, the entire journey of the human experience begins with these words "in the beginning God created the heavens and the earth" (Genesis 1:1 KJV). It says further that "and God said let there be" as the tool of His creation (Genesis KJV). So we should use our words to let positive things begin for us. Let there be positive words in your life today by using good words with the good people around you. Go get them, Christian!

PRE-THOUGHT:

I will choose my words carefully to ensure they uplift and encourage others.

NOTES

THE BOUNCE

GROUP TALK

Ana Paula Frezatto Martins, a physical education teacher in Brazil, arranged her class in a circle around two cups of sealed grains. To one cup, the students were asked to say negative things such as, "You are useless," and "You can't accomplish anything." To the second glass, the kids were asked to say positive things such as, "You are special," "You can accomplish anything," and "You are smart." Martins then put the rice cups aside, and when the kids checked on them on a later day, the rice in the "love cup" had fermented, while the rice in the "hate cup" had become dark and moldy. This experiment led many students to be more positive in their daily lives.

Ten-year-old Anita Santini Trevisan said, "When you say something nice, like 'You can do it,' you feel that in your heart." Henrique Kloster said, "The damage of negativity is bigger than we can imagine. There are two ways to say things. The right way is to praise the good side of others with the eyes of the heart, not the eyes we see." Masaru Emoto was the originator of this rice experiment. He also performed a similar experiment testing distilled water and natural water frozen into crystals and exposed to different human emotions. "In all of these experiments," Emoto wrote, "The result was that we always observed beautiful crystals after giving good words, playing good music, and showing, playing, or offering prayer to water. On the other hand, we observed disfigured crystals in the opposite situation." [15]

THE PASTOR'S PERSPECTIVE

KEY VERSE

- *"An hypocrite with his mouth destroyeth his neighbour: but through knowledge shall the just be delivered."* (Proverbs 11:9 KJV)
- *"A good man out of the good treasure of his heart bringeth forth that which is good; and an evil man out of the evil treasure of his heart bringeth forth that which is evil: for of the abundance of the heart his mouth speaketh."* (Luke 6:45 KJV)
- *"He that keepeth his mouth keepeth his life: but he that openeth wide his lips shall have destruction."* (Prov 13:3 KJV)
- *"A wholesome tongue is a tree of life: but perverseness therein is a breach in the spirit."* (Prov 15:4 KJV)
- *"Therefore whatsoever ye have spoken in darkness shall be heard in the light; and that which ye have spoken in the ear in closets shall be proclaimed upon the housetops."* (Luke 12:3 KJV)
- *"But I say unto you, That every idle word that men shall speak, they shall give account thereof in the day of judgment."* (Matthew 12:36 KJV)

The concept is really quite simple. Your heart is deceitful and desperately wicked; left to its own devices, it will think there are clouds and rain even when the sky is blue and sunny. The "misconception of intent" can bring us to a place where we use words like daggers. We use them to repeatedly stab the people that we have pledged to love and support with our vows in a marriage, through giving birth to children, to those who are our neighbors, or by God's will against those who are fellow church members.

The repeated rice in a jar experiment has proven that words and the intention of the human heart projected through those words literally have the power to destroy living matter! If words have that kind of authority and nature, consider what you have done to those you are responsible for loving through the eyes of God.

Some of you say, "It is the other person's fault that I am angry, frustrated, or using these words." The reality is that nothing stays in your heart unless you allow it to, and you shall be judged for everything that escapes your lips. I say to all of us! Before we go, one word, father, that we repent. To clarify, before you say another word of destructive intent, stop speaking, and right now, where you are, repent of your words at this moment of revelation! Repentance is not for the other person to feel good, but you can feel whole! Repentance tells God that you are sorry for murdering love, destroying people, and derailing those closest to you. Again, repent before saying one more word; make peace with God in Jesus' name.

Those of you need no repentance because your words have been fitly spoken, and you have a disciplined tongue. Take a moment now to commit that you will continue in your path of saying only life-giving words to those closest to you.

Come on, Christian, you've got this. We have an opportunity to repent and redirect our words while we're still breathing. Our terms matter when we thoughtfully consider our eternal destination. Speak life.

PRE-THOUGHT:

When I encounter a relationship problem, I will thoughtfully steer the conversation in a positive direction.

NOTES

THE BOUNCE

WORDS REHEARSED
MAKE THINGS BETTER
. . . OR WORSE

Ikea demonstrated the power of words by using two of their plants for a social experiment with the intent to raise awareness of the effects of bullying. For 30 days, two plants were placed in a school and subjected to two identical environments. The only difference being one plant was situated near recordings of positive words. The other was bombarded by negative comments. After 30 days, the "bullied" plant started wilting, while the complimented plant flourished!

If you were put into an fMRI scanner, a type of imaging system that can take a video of the neural changes in your brain, and saw the word "NO" on the screen faster than you could even realize, your brain would release dozens of stress-producing hormones. These chemicals interrupt the processes in your brain, which impairs logic, reason, language processing, and communication. Simply glancing at a list of negative words can make an anxious or depressed person feel worse. The more you play them over in your brain, the more you can damage the structures that regulate your memory, feelings, and emotions. This will disrupt your sleep, appetite, and even your ability to experience happiness.

When talking to others, if you verbalize negativity or even slightly frown, more stress chemicals are released in your brain and the listener's brain. They will then have higher anxiety and be more irritable, making it harder to cooperate and trust. Even simply gathering with people of a negative mindset can increase prejudices in your own mind. Any form of negative thinking will release destructive chemicals into your brain. This is especially true with children. The more negative words they hear, the more likely they will be highly anxious and stressed later in life. However, if you lead in positivity, your children will lead a much more productive life.

Negative thinking is also self-fulfilling. The more negative thought space you use in your mind, the harder it is to stop. But when those thoughts are verbalized through anger, the damage is far worse. Anger sends alarm messages through an angry person's brain that interfere with the decision-making frontal lobe, increasing the likelihood of acting irrationally. Words like poverty, illness, death, and divorce provoke fear, which stimulates specific chemicals in the brain that have an overall negative impact. Even if these thoughts are fantasies, the thalamus (sends sensory information) and the amygdala (deals with emotions) react as though the ideas were real. This makes it seem like the human brain is designed to worry. But we can take steps to prevent a negative spiral by stopping and asking ourselves if this threat is real or perceived. If it's not, you've just interrupted the amygdala's reaction. This then reduces the likelihood that your memory will retain the negativity. [27]

THE PASTOR'S PERSPECTIVE

KEY VERSE

- *"Keep back thy servant also from presumptuous sins; let them not have dominion over me: then shall I be upright, and I shall be innocent from the great transgression. Let the words of my mouth, and the meditation of my heart, be acceptable in thy sight, O Lord, my strength, and my redeemer."* (Psalm 19:13-14 KJV)

KEY DEFINITION

- Pre·sump·tu·ous (adjective) - (of a person or their behavior) failing to observe the limits of what is permitted or appropriate

The experiments and articles above tell us that those in secular society are discovering what the word of God has directed us to for millennia. People who claim to be Christian for many years of our lives believe we have some sort of dispensation that allows us as individuals to be outside of the Commandments or the guidelines in God's Word. We treat each other poorly, think negative thoughts about people all day long, and gossip with other people concerning things we don't truly understand, nor have any right to share our opinions. We destructively move through relationships, leaving a trail of brokenness, despair, and bad feelings behind us. All because we presume that we're okay.

In Psalm 19, David indicates that a person pursuing the God of the Bible should be concerned about being presumptuous. The only way to be saved from the sin of presuming we're above the law or have a right to demonstrate negativity is to check our attitude at the door and begin to be "acceptable in thy sight, O Lord," with the thoughts we think and the words we say (Psalm 19:14).

In the previous study, we read about how human beings will be judged for every idle word. However, we continue to spew venom, darkness, and anxiety-laden terms out of our mouths toward the children of the Lord, such as ourselves, spouses, children, and others. I don't want to be offensive, but shame on the husband who speaks or thinks negatively about his wife. Shame on your wife if you believe you have a right to tear down your husband in private or, what would be considered worse by God, tearing down a father in the presence of his children. Shame on any young person if you use destructive words or allow gossip magazines to be your meditation.

The real issue is that we don't value the very thing that took Him to the cross. The people, the relationships that they have with themselves and their neighbors. I have committed a presumptuous sin if I tear into another human being with my negative thoughts or words. I caused the person who was the target of my words to be less than adequate at loving themselves. Therefore less effective in loving their neighbor. Am I really irrational to think I can tear people down and the Lord will build me up? Like Toby Mac says, "Speak life ... speak hope, speak love." [25].

Today, you can think you are happy, speak yourself into joy, or choose to not think yourself happy. However, the excuses come out: "You don't understand how hard it is," "The history of my life tells me that I should be negative," "I've had a callous life," etc. If you think life is tough, can you imagine eternity separated from the Lord? This thought should cause you to truly repent of those things that have happened to you and through you. Begin right now to speak positively. My friend Charles Robinson once said, "Eternity is a long time to be wrong." Come on, Christian, don't just think about it; act on it. Speak something positive right now before you go one more step in your life! Before you take one more breath. Even if it is just into the air toward God, think a positive thought and speak a positive word. Repent or perish is the way that Jesus put it. Even though we won't know who is missing, Heaven will be a lonely place without you (for you).

To leave you with this last thought, why do we say "I do" to relationships, friendships, and even experiences with God. Then, spend the rest of our time tearing people down and destroying what He is trying to build. I recommend we change, and we change now! Take a minute and say something good now, think something good now, and reach out to the people around you with good words. Don't hesitate, do it now! Literally, stop what you're doing. Now, text a positive message, speak a positive word right now, and begin on the first step to a brand new you.

PRE-THOUGHT:

By controlling the thoughts that replay in my mind, I can express a positive word just in time.

NOTES

BIBLIOGRAPHY

1. Abello, Joan Cyril. "11 Signs You Are Prideful: How to Get Rid of Pride in Your Heart." Inspiring Tips, 31 July 2019, https://inspiringtips.com/signs-you-are-prideful-how-to-get-rid-of-pride/

2. Abrams, Allison. "The Psychology of Hate." Psychology Today, Sussex Publishers, 9 Mar. 2017, www.psychologytoday.com/us/blog/nurturing-self-compassion/201703/the-psychology-hate

3. American Physiological Society. "Mind over matter: Can you think your way to strength?" ScienceDaily. ScienceDaily, 31 December 2014. https://www.sciencedaily.com/releases/2014/12/141231154012.htm

4. Amodeo, John. "Why Pride Is Nothing to Be Proud Of." Psychology Today, Sussex Publishers, 06 Jun. 2015, https://www.psychologytoday.com/intl/blog/intimacy-path-toward-spirituality/201506/why-pride-is-nothing-be-proud?amp

5. "Anger." Psychology Today, Sussex Publishers, https://www.psychologytoday.com/us/basics/anger

6. "Anxiety Disorders: Types, Causes, Symptoms & Treatments." Cleveland Clinic, 2017, https://my.clevelandclinic.org/health/diseases/9536-anxiety-disorders

7. Barron, Carrie. "False Accusations, Scapegoats, and the Power of Words." Psychology Today, Sussex Publishers, 17 Feb. 2014, https://www.psychologytoday.com/us/blog/the-creativity-cure/201402/false-accusations-scapegoats-and-the-power-words

8. Bergland, Christopher. "Scientists Find That a Single Word Can Alter Perceptions." PsychologyToday, Sussex Publishers, 27 Aug. 2013, https://www.psychologytoday.com/us/blog/the-athletes-way/201308/scientists-find-single-word-can-alter-perceptions

9. Carter, Sherrie Bourg. "Emotions Are Contagious-Choose Your Company Wisely." Psychology Today, Sussex Publishers, 20 Oct. 2012, https://www.psychologytoday.com/us/blog/high-octane-women/201210/emotions-are-contagious-choose-your-company-wisely

10. D'Amato, Erik. "Mystery of Disgust." Psychology Today, Sussex Publishers, 1 Jan. 1998, https://www.psychologytoday.com/us/articles/199801/mystery-disgust

11. Devaney, Jacob. "Science Validates Collective Intention." UPLIFT, 16 Jan. 2020, https://uplift.love/science-validates-collective-intention/

12. Eddy, Bill. "Five Types of High-Conflict Personalities." Psychology Today, Sussex Publishers, 6 Nov. 2017, https://www.psychologytoday.com/us/blog/5-types-people-who-can-ruin-your-life/201711/five-types-high-conflict-personalities#:~:text=They%20all%20have%20the%20basic,traits%20of%20five%20personality%20disorders.

13. Fields, R. Douglas. "Humans Are Genetically Predisposed to Kill Each Other." PsychologyToday, Sussex Publishers, 2 Oct. 2016, https://www.psychologytoday.com/us/blog/the-new-brain/201610/humans-are-genetically-predisposed-kill-each-other

14. Firestone, Lisa. "The Value of Sadness." Psychology Today, Sussex Publishers, 30 Jul., 2015, https://www.psychologytoday.com/us/blog/compassion-matters/201507/the-value-sadness#:~:text=As%20my%20father%2C%20psychologist%20and,ourselves%20and%20even%20more%20resilient.

15. Freitas, Joao. "Teacher Shows Students How Negative Words Can Make Rice Moldy." Good News Network, 11 June 2017, https://www.goodnewsnetwork.org/teacher-shows-students-how-negative-words-makes-rice-moldy/

16. Fuller, Kristen. "The Difference Between Sadness and Depression." Psychology Today, Sussex Publishers, 17 Oct. 2019. www.psychologytoday.com/us/blog/happiness-is-state-mind/201910/the-difference-between-sadness-and-depression

17. Gordon, Richard. "Mind Over Matter: 4 Cutting-Edge Scientific Experiments Proving Your Mind Affects Physical Reality." Conscious Lifestyle Magazine, 22 Apr. 2019, https://www.consciouslifestylemag.com/mind-over-matter-experiments/

18. Hendel, Hilary Jacobs. "Disgust: A Natural Emotional Response to Abuse." Psychology Today, Sussex Publishers, 14 Oct. 2019, https://www.psychologytoday.com/us/blog/emotion-information/201910/disgust-natural-emotional-response-abuse

19. Hillin, Taryn. "Science Explains Why Surprise Brings Us Pleasure." Splinter, Splinter, 1 Apr. 2015, https://splinternews.com/science-explains-why-surprise-brings-us-pleasure-1793846784

20. "Intentionality." Oxford English and Spanish Dictionary, Thesaurus, and Spanish to English Translator, Lexico, 2020, www.lexico.com/definition/intentionality.

21. Kets de Vries, Manfred. "Seven Signs of the Greed Syndrome." INSEAD Knowledge, INSEAD, 8 Apr. 2016, https://knowledge.insead.edu/blog/insead-blog/seven-signs-of-the-greed-syndrome-4624

22. Lancer, Darlene. "Do You Trust Too Much or Too Little?" Psychology Today, Sussex Publishers, 11 Dec. 2019, www.psychologytoday.com/us/blog/toxic-relationships/201912/do-you-trust-too-much-or-too-little

23. Lockwood, Jeffery. "The Making of Disgust." Psychology Today, Sussex Publishers, 02 Jun. 2016, https://www.psychologytoday.com/us/blog/the-infested-mind/201606/the-making-disgust

24. Maron, Dina Fine. "Why Words Matter: What Cognitive Science Says about Prohibiting Certain Terms." Scientific American, Springer Nature Division, 19 Dec. 2017, www.scientificamerican.com/article/why-words-matter-what-cognitive-science-says-about-prohibiting-certain-terms/

25. McKeehan, Toby. "Speak Life." Eye On It, ForeFront Records, 2012. https://open.spotify.com/track/7FO6QgfJRKtEwZiYO0dIO9?si=894343521d9b4a37

26. Nayar, Vineet. "The Power of Intent." Harvard Business Review, 18 Feb. 2013, https://hbr.org/2013/02/the-power-of-intent.

27. Newberg, Andrew, and Mark Waldman. "Why This Word Is So Dangerous to Say or Hear." Psychology Today, Sussex Publishers, 1 Aug.2012, www.psychologytoday.com/us/blog/words-can-change-your-brain/201208/why-word-is-so-dangerous-say-or-hear

28. Nightingale, Earl. "The Strangest Secret – Earl Nightingale: Video and Transcript." IMPACT CM Ltd, 12 June 2017, www.impactcm.co.uk/2015/03/the-strangest-secret-earl-nightingale-video-and-transcript/

29. "Panic Disorder & Panic Attacks; Symptoms, Causes, Treatment." Cleveland Clinic, 2018, Panic Attacks: Panic Disorder, Anxiety Disorder, Symptoms, Causes (clevelandclinic.org)

30. Patel, Neil. "The Psychology of Anticipation and What It Means for Your Conversions." Unbounce, 14 July 2014, https://unbounce.com/conversion-rate-optimization/psychology-of-anticipation-conversion-rates/

31. Persaud, Raj. "Who Murders Children? the Latest Research Profiles Child Killers, but Can It Help Detection?" *HuffPost UK*, HuffPost UK, 9 Dec. 2012, https://www.huffingtonpost.co.uk/dr-raj-persaud/child-protection_b_1950749.html

32. "Positive Psychology and the Science of Happiness." Pursuit of Happiness, 2018, https://www.pursuit-of-happiness.org/science-of-happiness

33. Powell, Alvin. "When Science Meets Mindfulness." Harvard Gazette, 9 Apr. 2018, https://news.harvard.edu/gazette/story/2018/04/harvard-researchers-study-how-mindfulness-may-change-the-brain-in-depressed-patients/

34. Radin, Dean et al. "Distant Healing Intention Therapies: An Overview of the Scientific Evidence." Global advances in health and medicine vol. 4, Suppl (2015): 67-71. https://journals.sagepub.com/doi/10.7453/gahmj.2014.019

35. Roberts, Martha. "The Joy of Anticipation." Psychologies, 8 Apr. 2014, https://www.psychologies.co.uk/the-joy-of-anticipation/

36. Saplakoglu, Yasemin. "What Does Sadness Look Like in the Brain?" Live Science, Future plc, 8 Nov. 2018, https://www.livescience.com/64043-sadness-brain-activity.html.

37. Tiller, William, and Jeff Rense. "How the Power of Intention Alters Matter." The Spirit of Ma'at, http://spiritofmaat.com/archive/mar2/tiller.htm.

38. Tiller, William A. "Institute for Psychoenergetic Science." William A Tiller Institute for Psychoenergetic Science, 2017, https://www.tillerfoundation.org/

39. Time Magazine. "Religion: The Power of the Brief Burst." Time, Time USA., 13 Apr. 1959, content.time.com/time/magazine/article/0,9171,810996,00.html

40. Walton, Alice G. "'Mind Over Matter' May Actually Work When It Comes To Health, Study Finds." Forbes, Forbes Magazine, 12 Dec. 2018, https://www.forbes.com/sites/alicegwalton/2018/12/12/mind-over-matter-may-actually-work-when-it-comes-to-health-study-finds/?sh=527420db7bd7

41. Weindling, Miranda. "The Science of Intention." UPLIFT, 13 June 2017, https://uplift.love/the-science-of-intention/

42. "What Is Cognition & Cognitive Behaviour." Cambridge Cognition, 19 Aug. 2015, https://www.cambridgecognition.com/blog/entry/what-is-cognition#:~:text=Cognition%20is%20defined%20as%20%27the,used%20to%20guide%20your%20behavior.

43. Wikipedia contributors. "False accusation." Wikipedia, The Free Encyclopedia. Wikipedia, The Free Encyclopedia, 27 Jun. 2020, https://en.wikipedia.org/wiki/False_accusation

44. Wikipedia contributors. "Lie." Wikipedia, The Free Encyclopedia. Wikipedia, The Free Encyclopedia, 24 July 2020, https://en.wikipedia.org/wiki/Lie

"My personal choice is to disengage from negative thoughts. To disengage from the belief that if I think negatively, I will receive a positive."

Happiness is something that many people feel eludes them. Most would be more than willing to have more of it in their lives. From work stresses, difficulties at home, or just a lack of understanding of one's place and purpose in the world, there are lots of problems borne of perspective or experience that keep all of us from reaching our full potential happiness in life. The author's thirty-day program gives readers a regular, brief activity of reflection and study of their emotions in order to better understand where they come from, how to manage those emotions, or, in the case of negative ones, reprogram them to become positive affirmations that serve a more realized purpose. With just a few minutes a day, readers can learn to reframe their thinking and let go of negative or self-defeating habits.

Each chapter begins by identifying and explaining a particular state of mind. Initially, this begins with simple emotions that everyone experiences, but the teaching eventually evolves into deeper lines of thinking, highlighting where a person's intentions come from, what leads to hatred and how to combat it, and finally, how to communicate more clearly and directly without causing emotional harm to others. From there, readers get a more ecclesiastical view of the matter and how it affects people without them necessarily realizing it. Appropriate scripture is quoted to offer inspiration, and finally, each chapter concludes with a "pre-thought" that supplants an ingrained style of thinking with a new idea or mantra that encourages the reader to be more active in their reactions to things and be mindful of the choices that they make.

What many readers may find refreshing and encouraging about this title compared to other self-help and inspirational readings is that the steps that are presented are all very simple, internal choices that a person can practice, write down, memorize, or just study to make massive changes. Rather than overhauling their life with new structures, habits, and activities, this plan provides simple perspective tweaks that can take a commonly experienced situation and make it feel brand new. Themes of personal accountability and growth are at the core of this text, and so the only requirement from the reader to incorporate these lessons is to make the effort of practicing and incorporating the pre-thoughts and Bible verses into situations that might have been emotionally charged before.

When emotions become overwhelming, and a person feels like they don't have control over their own thoughts, the immediate feeling can be hopelessness, frustration, or even fear. While there's no surefire way to ease that burden for every person, what is possible can often be complicated by accessibility and resources. For that reason, a method like this one that simply retrains a person's reflexive thinking into something that is more empathetic, reflective, and responsible is an ideal solution that anyone can attempt.

While every situation and challenge is unique, and no two people are alike, the principles and emotional foundations of this book and this program are something that anyone can access and work on, and for that reason, it can either function as a great place to begin one's journey of improvement or a low-risk, lowcost alternative when other methods may not be offering the desired results. Walters has produced a useful and unique guide that can help change the emotional course of one's life, steering the reader into more positive waters.

— Michael Radon
USRB

www.ingramcontent.com/pod-product-compliance
Lightning Source LLC
Chambersburg PA
CBHW041512120626
46551CB00018B/2403